DINOSAUR
SURVIVAL GUIDE

CLARE HIBBERT

ARCTURUS

Picture Credits:
Key: b-bottom, t-top, c-center, l-left, r-right
Stefano Azzalin: 8-9, 10-11, 16-17, 22-23, 24-25, 62-63, 66tr, 67tl, 67bl, 67cr, 69tr, 72l, 73t, 75tl, 81tr, 82cl, 86, 89tc, 91tr, 95br, 96-97, 98-99, 102cl, 102cr, 104-105, 106tr, 106br, 109cr, 110-111, 114-115, 118-119, 120-121, 122-123, 124-125; **Martin Bustamente:** 4-5, 7bl, 20-21, 26bl, 26c, 26br, 27cl, 28-29, 30cl, 30b, 31tl, 31tr, 31cl, 32-33, 34-35, 36-37, 38-39, 40-41, 44-45, 46tr, 46bl, 48-49, 50-51, 52-53, 56l, 57tl, 57bl, 60-61, 64-65, 66bl, 67tr, 70cr, 71tl, 71bl, 71br, 76-77, 78-79, 82-83, 93tl, 93bl, 106bl, 107, 112-113, 116-117; **Juan Calle:** 12tr, 12br, 13tl, 18cl, 19br, 87bl, 100-101, 109c, 121cl, 125tr; **Genkis:** 93tr; **Colin Howard:** 20bl, 70cl, 71tr; **Kunal Kundu:** 54-55, 58-59, 68-69, 72-73, 74-75, 80-81, 88-89; **Jerry Pyke:** 6c, 6br, 7bl, 9tl, 10bl, 14bl, 16tl, 17tl, 22l, 24br, 26tr, 32cl, 35bl, 37bl, 41tl, 42c, 45t, 46br, 47tl, 47bl, 49tr, 50cr, 52bl, 55br, 59tl, 60bl, 64br, 68cl; **Shutterstock:** cover (DM7, Elenamiv, Lightspring, Dudarev Mikhail, rayuken and rodho), icons (Ecelop and CHNSWR), hazard strips (benchart), backgrounds (Thomas Bethge, chaoss, Dashikka, Kasha-malasha, Miloje and photoff), 5tr (Sergei Drozd), 7tl (Marques), 13bl (Michael Rosskothen), 13br (Chase Clausen), 18bc (Michael Rosskothen), 18br (DM7), 19tl (DM7), 19tr (DM7), 25cr (Artur Synenko), 27tr (DM7), 29tr (Lefteris Papaulakis), 36cr (AuntSpray), 43tl (33333), 44tr (SJ Travel Photo and Video), 47br (Talvi), 54cb (Ihor Pasternak), 58tr (Catmando), 59br (Aleksey Stemmer), 80c (Enlightened Media), 85tl (Ozja), 87tl (Andreas Meyer), 92l (Michael Rosskothen), 92r (Catmando), 94br (Witty bear), 97bl (Rosa Jay), 99bl (John Nairne), 105t (Mopic), 114bl (Gemenacom); **Parwinder Singh:** 5br, 7tr, 9br, 11r, 15tl, 16l, 21r, 23r, 27tr, 28bl, 31b, 33tr, 34l, 36b, 38b, 40bl, 47tr, 48bl, 50b, 53bl, 57br, 61r, 62b, 65t, 66b, 69b, 70bl, 74bl, 77b, 79b, 83tr, 84-85, 87br, 89br, 90bl, 93br, 97tr, 100br, 103r, 107b, 109t, 111r, 112bl, 117t, 119br, 121tr, 123tr, 125b; **Val Walerczuk:** 4r, 6bl, 14-15, 30cr, 42-43, 56r, 81br, 87br, 90-91, 94-95, 102-103, 108-109; **Wikimedia Commons:** 13tr (FunkMonk/Muséum national d'Histoire naturelle, Paris), 27br (Daderot/Houston Museum of Natural Science), 41br (Haplochromis), 77tr (Allie Caulfield/Los Angeles Museum of Natural History), 83br (Elapied), 88bl (Natural History Museum, London), 113bl (Craig Pemberton/Museum of Northern Arizona).

ARCTURUS

This edition published in 2016 by Arcturus Publishing Limited
26/27 Bickels Yard, 151–153 Bermondsey Street,
London SE1 3HA

Copyright © Arcturus Holdings Limited

ISBN: 978-1-78404-953-9
CH004772NT
Supplier 26, Date 0116, Print Run 4544

Author: Clare Hibbert
Editors: Joe Harris and Clare Hibbert @ Hollow Pond
Designer: Amy McSimpson @ Hollow Pond

Printed in China

DINOSAUR SURVIVAL GUIDE

SURVIVAL IN DINOSAUR TIMES 4

SURVIVAL IN DINOSAUR TIMES

CHANGING CONTINENTS

During the Mesozoic, the world changed a lot. Around 230 mya, in the Triassic, the land was clumped into one big supercontinent. Slowly, at a rate of about 2 cm (0.8 in) a year, the land broke up to form today's continents.

This is how the world looked during the Cretaceous period:

This book is all about how to survive in dinosaur times. In reality, humans did not appear until more than 50 million years after the last dinosaurs died out. But imagine if you could travel back in time. Would you have what it took to survive?

Dinosaurs lived on the Earth during the Mesozoic era, a long span of time that lasted from 250 to 65 million years ago (mya). Scientists break this down into three slightly shorter periods:

Triassic period: 250 mya to 208 mya

Jurassic period: 208 mya to 145 mya

Cretaceous period: 145 mya to 65 mya

Dinosaurs appeared during the Triassic. They died out at the end of the Cretaceous, along with other life forms including pterosaurs (flying lizards) and plesiosaurs (long-necked sea monsters).

Triceratops

Diplodocus

No one knows how many kinds of dinosaur there were. So far, scientists have named around 700 species—but there could be just as many left to discover!

Pterosaur

DINO SURVIVAL ESSENTIALS

Imagine if you were about to set out on an adventure in the Mesozoic era. What would you take with you?

One important piece of kit would be a compass. When exploring unknown terrain, a compass is essential—especially if you may need to go off-course to shake off a hungry T. rex!

T. rex

Parasaurolophus

SURVIVAL GUIDE: DINOSAURS

The blue guides in this book will give you tips about how to survive both dinosaurs and other prehistoric hazards. There's no point escaping a raging dinosaur only to tumble over a cliff!

CHAPTER ONE: KILLER BEASTS

In this chapter, you will meet some of the deadliest dinosaurs that ever walked the Earth. Many of these meat-eating monsters are armed with slashing claws and bone-crushing jaws. You'll also encounter other scary reptiles that are close cousins of the dinosaurs.

Experts divide dinosaurs into two main groups, based on their hip bones. Ornithischian (bird-hipped) dinosaurs are all plant-eaters. Saurischian (lizard-hipped) dinosaurs include plant-eating sauropods and meat-eating theropods. The only dinosaurs you will encounter in this chapter are terrifying, meat-eating theropods.

Watch out for savage early crocs in this chapter. Like their dinosaur cousins, they are carnivores (meat-eaters).

SEE PAGES 24–25

Allosaurus lives in the Late Jurassic, 155 to 150 mya. It ranges all over North America, but has also been discovered in Europe and East Africa.

Like its cousin T. rex, tough guy Tarbosaurus lives at the end of the Cretaceous. And like T. rex, this dinosaur has surprisingly puny arms!

Before dinosaurs rule, predatory reptiles are top of the pile. This one, Proterosuchus, lives in the Early Triassic.

SEE PAGES 14–15

SEE PAGES 8–9

JUST BEFORE THE AGE OF THE DINOSAURS THERE WAS A MASS EXTINCTION.

MANY SPECIES ALL DIED OUT AT ONCE.

ALL CHANGE!

The process of species slowly changing, new species appearing and old ones becoming extinct (dying out) is called evolution. It happens because certain individuals have characteristics that give them more chance of survival. For example, a T. rex with powerful jaws will get more food than a weak-jawed one, and be more likely to have babies. Over time, the species changes—more of the individuals have powerful jaws.

SURVIVAL GUIDE: KILLER BEASTS

Carry a steak in your bag to chuck in the opposite direction if any carnivore fancies a taste of you. Keep it well wrapped, though—otherwise the smell of the meat will attract hungry hunters!

Tyrannosaurus rex (T. rex for short) is the most famous, and scary, dinosaur of all time! It lives at the very end of the dinosaur era.

Acrocanthosaurus's huge size is matched by its massive appetite. This big beast is never fussy—it will eat any old meat.

SEE PAGES 20–21

SEE PAGES 16–17

CREEPY CARNIVORE

Early in the Triassic, dinosaurs are not the main hunters. Proterosuchus, which is about the size of a grown man, is one of the largest predators of its day. It hunts on land and also in the water.

Just like modern crocodiles, Proterosuchus is an ambush predator. It lurks by a lake or river, waiting for animals to come to drink. Its preferred prey is dog-sized Lystrosaurus, a weird reptile that looks like a cross between a pig and a lizard.

Lystrosaurus has come to drink by the river.

Today's largest crocodiles are about four times longer than Proterosuchus.

ARCHOSAURS

Proterosuchus is an early archosaur (say "ark-o-saw"), or "ruling reptile." Crocodiles and birds are archosaurs. The group also includes pterosaurs, dinosaurs, and extinct crocodilians such as Proterosuchus. Archosaurs' skulls all have a hole between the eye socket and nostril and another near the back of the lower jaw.

Long, hooked snout.

BEASTLY DATA

PROTEROSUCHUS (PRO-TEH-RO-SU-KUSS)
MEANING: "EARLIER CROCODILE"

HEIGHT: 1 M (3.3 FT)
LENGTH: 1.9 M (6 FT)
WEIGHT: 90 KG (200 LB)

FAMILY: PROTEROSUCHIDAE
TIME: EARLY TRIASSIC
DIET: FISH, SMALL REPTILES

SURVIVAL GUIDE:
PROTEROSUCHUS

If you are ever faced by a Proterosuchus, run away! If you're unlucky enough to be ambushed and dragged into the water, don't struggle. Poke the hideous hunter in the eyes or on the nose instead.

Curved teeth for gripping prey.

ACE ARCHOSAUR

Bony plates along back, like a crocodile's.

Postosuchus is the main predator in Late Triassic North America. Although it looks like a very primitive theropod, it belongs to a different family (the rauisuchians). It lives alongside dinosaurs, though, and it hunts them—as well as crocodiles and any other animals that cross its path.

Postosuchus relies on its huge size to overpower prey. Its skull is massive, too, and its strong jaws are packed with sharp, serrated teeth. The longest teeth are more than 7 cm (2.8 in) long and perfectly designed for tearing through flesh.

Sharp, dagger-like teeth for tackling large prey.

The first Postosuchus fossils were mistaken for the dinosaur Coelophysis.

BEASTLY DATA

POSTOSUCHUS (POST-OH-SU-KUSS)
MEANING: "CROCODILE FROM POST (A CITY IN TEXAS)"

FAMILY: RAUISUCHIDAE
TIME: MIDDLE TO LATE
      TRIASSIC
DIET: MEAT

HEIGHT: 1.2 M (3.9 FT)
LENGTH: 4 M (13 FT)
WEIGHT: 565 KG
        (1,250 LB)

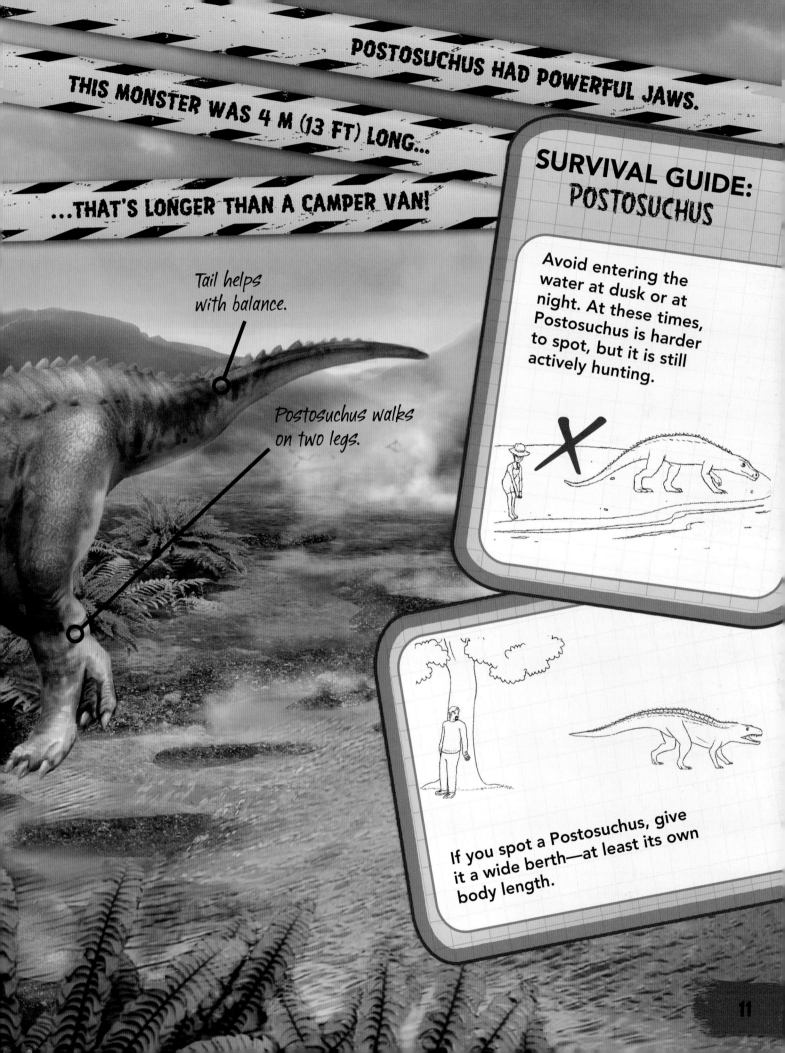

Tail helps with balance.

Postosuchus walks on two legs.

SURVIVAL GUIDE: POSTOSUCHUS

Avoid entering the water at dusk or at night. At these times, Postosuchus is harder to spot, but it is still actively hunting.

If you spot a Postosuchus, give it a wide berth—at least its own body length.

11

FREAKY FISH EATERS

Weird-looking dinosaurs prowl by the river. Baryonyx, Irritator, Ichthyovenator, and Cristatusaurus all belong to the spinosaur family. These dinosaurs scan the water for prey with gleaming, beady eyes. When they spot a fish, they dart down and grab it.

DINO DISCOVERY

Baryonyx was found in 1983. Amateur fossil hunter William Walker was at a clay pit in Surrey, England, when something caught his eye. A big claw was sticking out of the side of the pit! It belonged to an almost complete skeleton of Baryonyx, a dinosaur that lived in the Cretaceous.

Baryonyx has an impressive 30-cm (12-in) claw on each hand, which it uses to hook fish.

FIELD NOTES

Bayonyx has 32 top teeth and 64 bottom teeth. They're finely serrated—just right for getting a firm grip on slippery fish.

A notch near the front of Baryonyx's upper jaw helps it to hold fish prey. The narrow skull is typical of a spinosaur.

BARYONYX HAS TWICE AS MANY TEETH AS T. REX!

Irritator is known from just one fossil head, which illegal traders "added to" so it would look more complete. The job of getting rid of the fake bits to reveal the real head was so annoying that the dinosaur was named Irritator!

This claw belongs to Bayonyx's cousin, Cristatusaurus, a spinosaur that lives in West Africa during the Early Cretaceous. Some dinosaur experts think it is the same beast as Suchomimus (see pages 122-123).

This spinosaur from Laos, Southeast Asia, is called Ichthyovenator, which means "fish hunter." It is up to 9 m (30 ft) long and has two separate sails on its back.

DANGER ZONE:
FAST-FLOWING RIVER

A prehistoric river is a dangerous place. Stay well back from the bank. Be especially careful after heavy rains when the river contains more water than usual. Then, even the strongest swimmer can easily be swept away

ALLOSAURUS

Allosaurus is probably the best-known predatory dinosaur after T. rex. This fearsome hunter is right at the top of the food chain. It terrorizes large plant-eaters—its bite marks have even been found in the spine of an Apatosaurus!

Allosaurus probably nests in packs but hunts alone. Its massive bulk makes it more than a match for its prey. It frequently takes on Stegosaurus, unfazed by its deadly tail spikes. It kills victims by slashing its teeth through their flesh. When its teeth break off or wear down, new ones grow in their place.

Allosaurus's skull is around 84 cm (2.8 ft) long!

Tail is outstretched for balance.

DINO DATA

ALLOSAURUS (AL-OH-SAWR-USS)
MEANING: "DIFFERENT LIZARD"

FAMILY: ALLOSAURIDAE
TIME: LATE JURASSIC
DIET: MEAT

HEIGHT: 5 M (16.5 FT)
LENGTH: 12 M (40 FT)
WEIGHT: 2.7 TONNES (3 TONS)

No matter how fast you are, you're unlikely to outrun Allosaurus. Your best bet is to find a good hiding place—fast! A hollow tree trunk is perfect.

SURVIVAL GUIDE:
ALLOSAURUS

Distinctive horns above the eyes.

Hatchet-like upper jaw.

Bite is not especially strong (it's weaker than a lion's).

Long claws for gripping prey.

ALLOSAURUS DISCOVERY

The first Allosaurus was discovered in 1877 in Colorado, USA. Its name means "different lizard" because its bones were unlike those of any other dinosaur fossils found so far. The bones had holes in them that made them lighter.

SPINY MONSTER

Crazy-looking Acrocanthosaurus is one of the largest theropods ever—it can weigh more than six tons! This lumbering heavyweight lives across North America, where it preys on sauropods and ankylosaurs.

Like its distant relative Allosaurus, Acrocanthosaurus uses its jaws (not its claws) to kill. Its big olfactory bulb (the part of its brain involved in smelling) gives it a brilliant sense of smell. This helps it hunt down live prey and also sniff out carrion to eat.

Long, heavy tail.

SURVIVAL GUIDE:
ACROCANTHOSAURUS

Acrocanthosaurus is a scavenger. To avoid becoming its next meal, distract it with some old carrion.

Short arms used for grabbing.

STORY OF THE SPINES

Acrocanthosaurus has a muscular ridge of spines along its neck, back, and tail. The spines are probably for showing off to attract a mate. Another possibility is that they help the dinosaur control its body temperature. A third idea is that the spines stiffen as Acrocanthosaurus rips into a victim's flesh, helping the predator to stay steady.

DINO DATA

ACROCANTHOSAURUS (ACK-ROH-CANTH-OH-SAWR-US)
MEANING: "HIGH-SPINED LIZARD"

FAMILY: CARCHARODONTOSAURIDAE
TIME: EARLY CRETACEOUS
DIET: MEAT

HEIGHT: 5.2 M (17 FT)
LENGTH: 12 M (39 FT)
WEIGHT: 6.2 TONNES
(6.8 TONS)

Tall spines along the back and tail.

Carrion (rotting meat).

Massive curved claw on each hand.

Acrocanthosaurus's 1.3-m (4.3-ft) long skull contains curved, knife-like teeth.

CRESTED HUNTERS

You can certainly spot these dangerous dinosaurs coming, thanks to their distinctive head crests. Dilophosaurus, Monolophosaurus, and Cryolophosaurus are all around during the Jurassic, but in completely different parts of the world.

Dilophosaurus lives in North America. Its name means "double-crested lizard." The two crests on its head probably help it to attract a mate—the female chooses the male with the showiest ones.

TETANURANS

Monolophosaurus is one of the earliest tetanurans, or stiff-tailed theropods. Its tail sticks out straight behind it, supported by a series of tendons, and is carried off the ground rather than trailing along it. Allosaurus and Tyrannosaurus are tetanurans, too.

Dilophosaurus feeds on fish and carrion. At around 6 m (20 ft) from head to tail and with a weight of about 455 kg (0.5 tons), it is one of the largest Early Jurassic dinosaurs.

Monolophosaurus is from China. It's likely that it hunts in packs. This trio is about to attack Einiosaurus.

Monolophosaurus means "single-crested lizard." The crest on its snout is hollow. It probably isn't used to amplify sounds like Parasaurolophus's (see pages 80-81). Being hollow simply stops it weighing down Monolophosaurus's head.

Cryolophosaurus is from Antarctica and South Africa. Its narrow skull makes it look a bit like a spinosaur. This big hunter is 6.5 m (21 ft) long and eats anything—carrion, fish, mammals, and other dinosaurs.

FIELD NOTES

Most theropod crests are parallel to the sides of the skull, but Cryolophosaurus's faces forward like a quiff! In fact, this dinosaur's nicknamed "Elvisaurus", after singer Elvis Presley who was famous for his quiff hairstyle.

IN CRYOLOPHOSAURUS'S TIME, ANTARCTICA ISN'T COVERED IN ICE!

TYRANT KING

Tyrannosaurus rex is one of the largest land carnivores that has ever lived. Experts disagree about whether it is an active hunter or simply a scavenger, but one thing is for sure—it has a stronger bite than any other animal.

T. rex's forward-facing eyes are one argument for it being an active hunter. They give it excellent depth perception, allowing it to see how near or far prey is. T. rex has muscly legs so it probably runs down its prey, specializing in taking slow-moving plant-eaters such as Triceratops or Edmontonia.

Stiff tail sticks out behind for balance.

Tyrannosaurus has different-sized teeth. The longest are about 15 cm (6 in).

DINO DATA

TYRANNOSAURUS REX (TIE-RAN-OH-SAWR-US RECKS)
MEANING: "KING OF THE TYRANT LIZARDS"

HEIGHT: 5.5 M (18 FT)
LENGTH: 12 M (39 FT)
WEIGHT: : 6.1 TONNES
(6.7 TONS)

FAMILY: TYRANNOSAURIDAE
TIME: LATE CRETACEOUS
DIET: MEAT

Mouth contains up to 58 serrated teeth.

Massive skull.

SURVIVAL GUIDE: TYRANNOSAURUS

T. rex might back down if you stand your ground and throw branches or stones at it. This technique definitely works against big cats... but would you be brave enough to risk trying it with a tyrannosaur?!

Very short arms.

Two large clawed fingers (there is a smaller third finger behind).

BULLISH BEAST

This freaky predator has even shorter arms than T. rex, but that's not its distinguishing feature. You can tell Carnotaurus by the pair of thick, 15-cm (6-in) horns over its eyes, like a bull's horns. The horns are for showing off to females and for fighting rival males in headbutting contests.

Long, muscular legs make Carnotaurus one of the speediest large theropods. Its 136-kg (300-lb) thigh muscles power it along after prey. It probably targets large, slow dinosaurs. Its killing technique is to hack at a victim over and over again with its upper jaw, which is lined with serrated teeth.

Short, deep skull with a broad snout.

Small, forward-facing eyes provide binocular vision.

DINO DATA

CARNOTAURUS (CAR-NO-TORE-US)
MEANING: "MEAT-EATING BULL"

FAMILY: ABELISAURIDAE
TIME: LATE CRETACEOUS
DIET: MEAT

HEIGHT: 3 M (10 FT)
LENGTH: 7.6 M (25 FT)
WEIGHT: 1,360 KG (1.5 TONS)

Carnotaurus has a relatively weak bite—but when it delivers lots of bites in quick succession, they are deadly.

Scaly, reptilian skin.

Short, puny arms.

SURVIVAL GUIDE: CARNOTAURUS

Carnotaurus's larger-than-usual caudal (tail) ribs help it to sprint but also make its tail too rigid for tight turns. Your best escape route is a twisty, turny one!

FIELD NOTES

Carnotaurus's skin is covered in lumpy, bumpy scales called osteoderms. Today's Mexican beaded lizards have these, too.

ALARMING LIZARD

Good sense of smell.

Sometimes nicknamed the Asian T. rex, Tarbosaurus is a close cousin of that North American predator. It has shorter arms, but a slightly longer skull. Scarily, Tarbosaurus has even more teeth in its jaw than T. rex —about 60 in total.

Tarbosaurus's hunting grounds are in Mongolia and elsewhere in China. It tracks down Saurolophus and other hadrosaurs, as well as sauropods, such as Nemegtosaurus. It also scavenges any dead carcasses it finds. Tarbosaurus's long, serrated teeth can easily crush through bone.

DINO DATA

**TARBOSAURUS (TAR-BO-SAWR-US)
MEANING: "ALARMING LIZARD"**

FAMILY: TYRANNOSAURIDAE
TIME: LATE CRETACEOUS
DIET: MEAT

HEIGHT: 4.5 M (15 FT)
LENGTH: 10 M (32 FT)
WEIGHT: 5.4 TONNES
(6 TONS)

Light covering of feathers.

Very short arms with sharp, curved claws.

LOCK JAW

Tarbosaurus's lower jawbone is designed to "lock" when biting into tough-skinned prey. Becoming rigid reduces the stress on the skull during the bite. The only other dinosaur with this locking mechanism is Tarbosaurus's close relative, Alioramus.

Tarbosaurus

Stiff tail for balance.

Big, sturdy feet.

DINO SURVIVAL ESSENTIALS

DAZZLING LIGHT

This basic piece of kit is essential for finding your way and avoiding danger if you are out and about in the dark. You can shine it directly into predators' eyes to distract and confuse them! Choose a solar-powered model so you don't have to carry spare batteries.

Some scientists think Tarbosaurus has a throat sac that it can puff up!

25

CHAPTER TWO: HUNTING DINOSAURS

In this chapter, you will meet an array of theropods—carnivorous dinosaurs than run on two legs. A few are solitary, but many of these efficient hunters team up in packs. Some theropods are giants, while others are not much more than 30 cm (1 ft) long.

Whatever their size, theropods all have sharp, serrated teeth. The first theropods, which live in the Late Triassic, are small and speedy meat-eaters. Walking and running on two legs frees up their front legs. They can use their "hands" to grip, and many species have slashing, killer claws.

Small and swift, Ornitholestes inhabits Late Jurassic North America. It is famous for its egg-stealing skills.

SEE PAGES 36–37

SEE PAGE 39

Troodon's small—just half the height of a man—but brainy. It might even be one of the smartest dinosaurs.

Like Troodon, Caudipteryx is a maniraptoran—a particular type of theropod known for its grasping hands.

Dromaeosaurs are theropods with deadly killer claws. The largest is Utahraptor, which lives in the Early Cretaceous.

SEE PAGE 38

SEE PAGES 40–41

SURVIVAL GUIDE: THEROPOD

Theropods rely on their excellent senses of smell, hearing, and sight to track prey. If you need to make a quick getaway, make a very loud noise to momentarily deafen and distract them.

Speedy Staurikosaurus is one of the first theropods. Like Herrerarasaurus (see pages 28–29), another early meat-eater, it has a clever sliding jaw.

SEE PAGE 31

Birds evolved from theropod dinosaurs.

FEATHERED THEROPODS

Until the 1990s, everyone thought that dinosaurs had scaly, reptilian skin. Then paleontologists found the first feathered theropod: Sinosauropteryx ("Chinese dragon wing"). How did feathers evolve? Perhaps reptile scales frayed at the edges, creating downy fluff that kept dinosaurs warm. Over time, the fluff evolved into feathers for display.

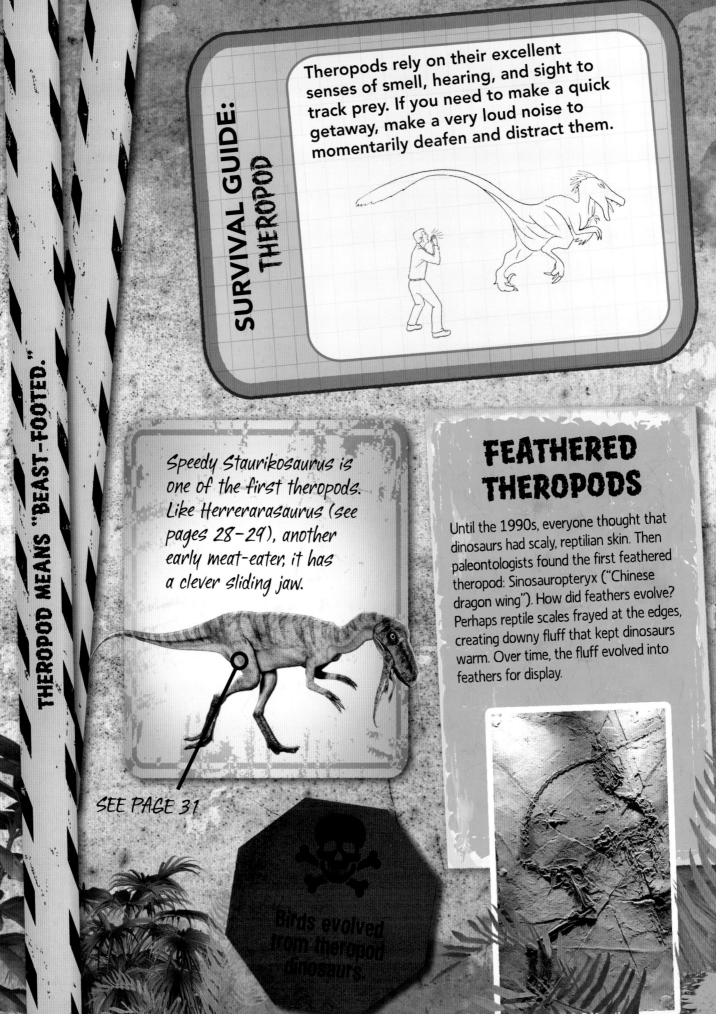

SWAMP THING

Long, narrow skull.

Herrerasaurus is one of the earliest, most primitive dinosaurs. It lives in the warm, swampy forests of Late Triassic South America. One of the largest hunters of the time, Herrerasaurus may go after its prey alone or in packs.

Sharp-eyed and with a fine sense of hearing, Herrerasaurus locates victims by sight and sound. It can easily outrun and overpower its prey. Its jaws are studded with backward-pointing teeth that can tear into flesh and pull it from the bone.

Lower jaw slides to deliver different kinds of bite, depending on the prey.

SURVIVAL GUIDE:
HERRERASAURUS

Herrerasaurus is unlikely to pick a fight with something huge. Carry a large stick and wave it around to make yourself look bigger.

PREY ANIMALS

Herrerasaurus feeds on small and medium-sized plant-eaters including small, stocky reptiles called rhynchosaurs and tusked primitive mammals called dicynodonts. It also hunts smaller dinosaurs, such as Pisanosaurus.

DINO DATA

HERRERASAURUS (HER-AIR-OH-SAWR-US)
MEANING: "HERRERA'S LIZARD"

FAMILY: HERRERASAURIDAE
TIME: LATE TRIASSIC
DIET: MEAT

HEIGHT: 1.5 M (5 FT)
LENGTH: 3 M (9.8 FT)
WEIGHT: 210 KG (460 LB)

Strong back legs.

Curved claws
for grasping.

The first Herrerasaurus specimen was discovered in 1959 in the Andes Mountains by a farmer called Victorino Herrera.

DEADLY DARTERS

Don't be fooled by the small size of these early dinosaurs! They are fast and fierce, with sharp teeth, dangerous claws and a will to kill. They hunt in gangs, because working together allows them to bring down bigger prey animals.

Eoraptor's name means "dawn hunter." It is called that because it lives at the dawn, or beginning, of the dinosaur age. It eats anything it can find, including lizards, worms, and fish.

Eoraptor is about the size of a human toddler—and as energetic as one, too! Its intelligence and agility make it a formidable hunter. Its mouth is packed with small, sharp teeth.

This 3-m (10-ft) long hunter is Coelophysis. It goes after lizards and other small prey, delivering slashing bites with blade-like teeth. It is also a cannibal—it eats its own young.

Staurikosaurus's name means "southern cross lizard." It is named after a cross-shaped constellation (star pattern) visible in the night sky in the southern half of the world.

A quick runner, Staurikosaurus tracks down primitive mammals, small lizards, and insects. It is probably a close cousin of Herrerasaurus, but it is smaller (about the size of a large dog).

Chindesaurus is another relative of Herrerasaurus. This small carnivore lives in southwestern North America and is up to 2.3 m (7.5 ft) long.

FIELD NOTES

Staurikosaurus's long tail has more than 40 vertebrae—it's held off the ground when the dinosaur runs.

SURVIVAL GUIDE
DEADLY DARTERS

There's no point running to escape these dinos—they are fast! Climb a tree and wait till they've run past you instead.

DANGEROUS DUO

Related to the much-smaller Coelophysis, Liliensternus is a large, ferocious predator that lives in Late Triassic Europe. Like Coelophysis, it has muscular back legs and is a powerful sprinter. It covers large distances, tracking down herds of plant-eaters.

One of the animals that Liliensternus hunts is almost twice its size! Plateosaurus is an ancestor of the later sauropods and grows up to 10 m (33 ft) long. Liliensternus also feeds on smaller dinosaurs and lizards, including dead carcasses. It has sharp, blade-like teeth.

Long, tapering tail.

Strong back legs.

DINO DATA

LILIENSTERNUS (LIL-EE-EN-SHTERN-US)
MEANING: "FOR LILIENSTERN"

FAMILY: COELOPHYSIDAE
TIME: LATE TRIASSIC
DIET: MEAT

HEIGHT: 2 M (6.6 FT)
LENGTH: 5.5 M (18 FT)
WEIGHT: 128 KG (280 LB)

Double crest similar to Dilophosaurus's (see page 18).

(see page 18).

SURVIVAL GUIDE: LILIENSTERNUS

Liliensternus likes to pick off stragglers. Be part of a group of other people or dinosaurs if you can, and make sure you stay in the middle.

Sharp teeth.

Liliensternus is the largest carnivore of its time. Its fin-like double crests may help it to recognize other members of its species.

Lizard carcass.

DINO DISCOVERY

A German paleontologist called Friedrich von Huene discovered the first Liliensternus fossil in 1934 (he also made a record-breaking number of other discoveries). Von Huene named his find after Hugo Rühle von Lilienstern, a German count. It was his way of thanking the count, who did lots to support paleontology, including opening a fossil museum in his castle.

HORNED HUNTER

Ceratosaurus is a pack hunter that lives in the Jurassic, sharing the same stomping grounds as Allosaurus and competing for the same prey. Gangs of three or four Ceratosaurus work together to take down large plant-eaters such as Iguanodon and Stegosaurus.

You can recognize Ceratosaurus by the distinctive horns on its head—a nose horn and two other horns in front of its eyes. These are probably too fragile to be weapons. Ceratosaurus uses its horns to show off to possible mates or frighten off potential rivals. It also has bony scales called osteoderms along its back.

Super-long teeth.

SURVIVAL GUIDE:
CERATOSAURUS

Swampy forest habitat.

Ceratosaurus is an ambush predator, so make sure you never drop your guard. If you spot one about to strike, sound your emergency whistle. The shock of the noise might throw the dinosaur off balance!

FIELD NOTES

Experts have found three different Ceratosaurus species, on three different continents.

Ceratosaurus's huge gape and long teeth inflict shark-like wounds.

Primitive, four-fingered hands.

DINO DATA

CERATOSAURUS (SIR-RAT-OH-SAWR-US)
MEANING: "HORNED LIZARD"

FAMILY: CERATOSAURIDAE
TIME: LATE JURASSIC
DIET: MEAT

HEIGHT: 4 M (13 FT)
LENGTH: 6 M (20 FT)
WEIGHT: 750 KG
(1,650 LB)

SMASH 'N' GRAB

Small, lightly built, and swift, Ornitholestes is a specialist egg robber. It also feeds on dinosaur hatchlings, frogs, lizards, and insects. Unless it is cornered, it is unlikely to attack any creature larger than itself, but it can inflict some nasty wounds while defending itself.

Ornitholestes probably hunts at night as well as by day. Its long tail, which makes up around half of its body length, helps it stay balanced as it speeds along. Ornitholestes has long arms for a theropod, with a wider-than-usual range of movement. This mobility means it's good at grabbing hold of prey or smashing into eggs.

SEIZING OPPORTUNITIES

Ornitholestes is often found around the edges of sauropod nesting sites, and even lays its own eggs here. It means that it is near a ready-source of food—protein-rich sauropod eggs and hatchlings.

SURVIVAL GUIDE: ORNITHOLESTES

Like all theropods, Ornitholestes uses its sense of smell when hunting. Stay upwind so that it can't sniff you out.

Filament-like feathers.

Ornitholestes' fine covering of feathers keeps its body warm.

Long, slender hands.

Sauropod egg.

DINO DATA

ORNITHOLESTES (AWN-EE-THOH-LEST-EEZ)
MEANING: "BIRD ROBBER"

HEIGHT: 70 CM (2.3 FT)
LENGTH: 2 M (6.6 FT)
WEIGHT: 13 KG (29 LB)

FAMILY: ORNITHOLESTINAE
TIME: LATE JURASSIC
DIET: MEAT

FEATHERED FIENDS

This group of theropods is called the maniraptorans, or "hand snatchers." One of their distinguishing features is their long arms with three-fingered hands designed for grabbing. These are some of the last dinosaurs that lived, and many are speedy hunters.

Ostrich-like Troodon lives in North America. Good binocular vision from its relatively large eyes helps Troodon to pinpoint the position of a range of different prey. It has a taste for baby hadrosaurs.

Not much larger than a chicken, Sinovenator is one of the smallest maniraptorans—but don't be fooled. Its sickle claws are designed for slashing and its lower jaw is crammed with masses of small, sharp teeth.

Beipiaosaurus has huge clawed hands —perfect for scratching insects from the bark of a tree. This dinosaur probably eats carrion, too. Its beak looks toothless, but Beipiaosaurus has hidden "cheek teeth."

SURVIVAL GUIDE: MANIRAPTORAN

Distract maniraptorans by dropping an item of clothing—while they pause to gather it up to line their nest, you can run away!

Oviraptor's name means "egg thief"—the first people to find one thought (wrongly) that it had stolen a Protoceratops's eggs. This dinosaur's toothless beak is strong enough to crack clam shells.

Turkey-sized Caudipteryx isn't a typical theropod, because it's not a carnivore. Its an omnivore. Its diet is mainly plants and seeds, though it probably eats insects, too. Watch out for its sharp, pointed beak!

WARM-BLOODED DINOSAURS

For a long time, paleontologists believed dinosaurs couldn't make their own body heat. They thought they were cold-blooded, like modern reptiles. Since the 1960s, many paleontologists have argued that some dinosaurs were warm-blooded (able to keep their bodies at a constant temperature), like modern birds and mammals.

Like Caudipteryx, Protarchaeopteryx lives in Cretaceous China. It's a similar size and has a similar diet, too. It's possible that it lives up in the trees, using its feathered arms to help it parachute from branch to branch.

3

PACK KILLERS

Like their dromaeosaur cousins, Utahraptors hunt in packs. Agile and intelligent, they work as a team to bring down prey. Once they get close, they pounce and make short work of their victim with their fearsome claws.

Utahraptors' big brains allow them to mastermind their hunting techniques. They have excellent binocular vision—like an eagle's—and can sniff out a meal from about 1.6 km (1 mile) away. They can even pick up low-frequency sounds, too.

Polar-bear-sized Utahraptor is the heavyweight of the dromaeosaurs.

SURVIVAL GUIDE:
UTAHRAPTOR

Never try and fist-fight a Utahraptor—those claws are deadly!

Deadly toe claws for stabbing prey in the jugular or spine.

Hand claws for slashing at prey.

DINO DATA

UTAHRAPTOR (YOO-TA-RAP-TOR)
MEANING: "UTAH'S THIEF"

FAMILY: DROMAEOSAURIDAE
TIME: EARLY CRETACEOUS
DIET: MEAT, FISH

HEIGHT: 3 M (9.8 FT)
LENGTH: 6 M (19.7 FT)
WEIGHT: 1 TONNE (1.1 TONS)

Jaw packed with razor-sharp teeth.

Short, muscular back legs launch Utahraptor into the air for its killer pounce.

KILLER CLAW

In common with other dromaeosaurs, Utahraptor has a killer claw on its second toe. It kicks this into its victim's vulnerable neck or spine. Even an enormous sauropod doesn't stand a chance when a pack of Utahraptors attacks!

RUNNING LIZARD

Deinonychus is another dromaeosaur that lives in Cretaceous North America. This wolf-sized predator uses its hooked toe claws to grip its unlucky victim while it bites the flesh with its slashing teeth. The claws are good to disembowel prey, too!

Deinonychus targets a range of prey animals, all plant-eaters larger than itself. It probably hunts in packs, working together to kill Iguanodon, Tenontosaurus, and even the occasional sauropod. The prey usually die of blood loss, after relentless biting from their killers.

Gaping jaw contains around 70 blade-like teeth.

DINO DATA

DEINONYCHUS (DIE-NON-EE-KUSS)
MEANING: "TERRIBLE CLAW"

FAMILY: DROMAEOSAURIDAE
TIME: EARLY CRETACEOUS
DIET: MEAT

HEIGHT: 1.2 M (4 FT)
LENGTH: 3.4 M (11.2 FT)
WEIGHT: 85 KG (187 LB)

Feathers for warmth and, possibly, display.

DINO SURVIVAL ESSENTIALS

UTILITY PENKNIFE

You won't survive in the wild without a penknife. Use a sharpening stone to keep it sharp and always clean the blade before you fold it away. A penknife is essential for building shelters, and for defending yourself, too.

Deinonychus might flap its forelimbs to keep its balance.

Sickle claw on second toe.

THE PERSON WHO FOUND THE FIRST DEINONYCHUS FOSSIL NAMED IT DAPTOSAURUS ("ACTIVE LIZARD"). THEN HE FORGOT TO TELL ANYONE ABOUT HIS DISCOVERY!

VICIOUS!

Velociraptor is Deinonychus's Asian cousin. One of the smaller dromaeosaurs, it is still deadly in combat—and speedy, too. It holds its second toe off the ground when it walks and runs, perhaps to make sure this killer claw never gets blunt.

Velociraptor lives in the Gobi Desert. The region is dry and sandy during the Cretaceous, just as it is today. It is home to herds of horned dinosaurs called Protoceratops. It is possible that Velociraptors treat Protoceratops as walking larders—snatching the odd bite from them, but not killing them.

DANGER ZONE: DESERT

The biggest danger in deserts is the lack of water. Carry supplies and drink at least eight glasses of water a day to make up for water lost by sweating. Travel at night or in the early morning, when it's cooler.

Protoceratops has become separated from its herd.

Velociraptors star in the film *Jurassic World*—but in fact this dinosaur lives after the Jurassic, in the Cretaceous.

DINO DATA

VELOCIRAPTOR (VEL-OSS-EE-RAPT-OR)
MEANING: "SPEEDY THIEF"

HEIGHT: 1 M (3.3 FT)
LENGTH: 2 M (6.6 FT)
WEIGHT: 15 KG (33 LB)

FAMILY: DROMAEOSAURIDAE
TIME: LATE CRETACEOUS
DIET: MEAT

FIELD NOTES

Its bird-like wrist can swivel, allowing Velociraptor to fold its arm against its body like a bird's wing.

Feathers for display and keeping warm.

Jaws have around 80 sharp teeth.

6.5-cm (2.6-in) long claw for holding down prey.

THERE IS A FAMOUS FOSSIL OF VELOCIRAPTOR AND PROTOCERATOPS.

THE PAIR ARE LOCKED IN COMBAT.

CHAPTER THREE: GIANT DINOSAURS

Prepare to encounter the giants of the dinosaur world. A few of the huge beasts in this chapter are carnivores, eager to get stuck into prey with their terrifying teeth. Most, though, are plant-eaters. They don't want to hunt you, but the sheer size of these lumbering monsters makes them incredibly dangerous.

The biggest dinosaurs are a group of plant-eaters called the sauropods. Like theropods, they belong to the lizard-hipped line of dinosaurs. Their distinctive, long necks allow them to reach up into trees for leaves. Their legs look like tree trunks —they have to be thick to support their bulky bodies.

Plateosaurus is an ancestor of the sauropods. It lives in Central and Northern Europe during the Late Triassic.

SEE PAGES 48–49

SEE PAGE 56

Brachiosaurus is a huge sauropod. Its name means "arm lizard" and was given to it because its "arms" (front legs) are longer than its back legs.

The enormous carnivore Spinosaurus is a theropod. Its distinguishing features are the crest along its back and its crocodile-like head.

SEE PAGES 58-59

Strange Placerias is a dicynodont—half-reptile, and half-mammal! This plant-eater of the Late Triassic has tusks to help it strip trees bare.

SEE PAGES 50–51

SEE PAGES 60–61

Therizinosaurus is armed with the freakiest talons ever seen! This theropod lives in the Late Cretaceous.

SURVIVAL GUIDE:
GIANT DINOSAUR

When faced with a giant, use your small size to your advantage—you can dash between the dinosaur's legs or easily hide out of sight!

MODERN GIANTS

The largest land animals today are mammals. Biggest of all is the African elephant. Males weigh an average of 5.5 tonnes (6 tons)—that's as much as a school bus! Like the sauropods of the past, elephants are vegetarians, but they can be extremely dangerous if they charge!

SAUROPOD MEANS "LIZARD-FOOTED."

EARLY GIANT

Herds of Plateosaurus roam through the forests of Europe during the Late Triassic. These animals, which belong to a group called the prosauropods, are ancestors of the sauropods. Unlike the sauropods, they stand on two legs, not four.

Being bipedal (standing on two legs) gives Plateosaurus an advantage over other early plant-eaters, because it can reach foods that are higher up. The dinosaur browses for food day and night, only resting for a while in the hot, middle part of the day

No one knows when—or if—Plateosaurus stops growing. Its growth rate speeds up or slows down, depending on the season.

SURVIVAL GUIDE:
PLATEOSAURUS

Plateosaurus will only attack if it's afraid. Look out for signs of fear and aggression, such as pawing at the ground or snorting.

Stocky back legs support Plateosaurus's body weight.

DINO DATA

PLATEOSAURUS (PLAY-TEE-OH-SAWR-USS)
MEANING: "BROAD LIZARD"

FAMILY: PLATEOSAURIDAE
TIME: LATE TRIASSIC
DIET: PLANTS

HEIGHT: 3 M (9.8 FT)
LENGTH: 7 M (22.9 FT)
WEIGHT: 1,800 KG
(4,000 LB)

Long skull.

Clawed hands for gathering food.

Rough, serrated teeth for grinding vegetation.

STUDYING PLATEOSAURUS

Since the first Plateosaurus fossil was found in 1834, the remains of more than 100 have been found. Plateosaurus is one of the most studied dinosaurs, but over the years scientists have come up with some outlandish theories. Some ignored the short length of its front legs and assumed it walked on all fours. One expert thought Plateosaurus hopped like a kangaroo!

49

HEAVY HIPPO

Weighing in at a couple of tonnes, Placerias is the hippopotamus of its day. This big beast is not a dinosaur but a dicynodont—a sort of cross between a reptile and a mammal. It is one of the Late Triassic's biggest plant-eaters.

Placerias browses on branches, leaves, and roots, cutting through plant matter with its sharp, beaky mouth. Like a hippo, it spends some of its time wallowing in shallow pools. Being part of a herd gives Placerias some protection against hungry predators. Sometimes, if the animals are spooked, they stampede!

BEASTLY DATA

PLACERIAS (PLA-SEER-EE-USS)
MEANING: "BROAD BODY"

HEIGHT: 1.6 M (5.3 FT)
LENGTH: 3.5 M (11.5 FT)
WEIGHT: 2 TONNES
(2.2 TONS)

FAMILY: STAHLECKERIIDAE
TIME: LATE TRIASSIC
DIET: PLANTS

SURVIVAL GUIDE: PLACERIAS

Watch out for Placerias's turtle-like beak as it can give a nasty nip. See the beast off with a homemade "spear"—a stick with a sharpened tip.

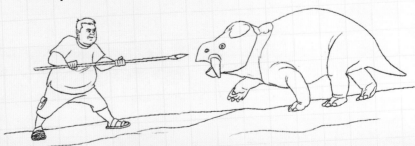

Stubby tail

Large tusks.

Turtle-like beak can slice through tough plant material.

Sturdy front legs.

PLACERIAS USES ITS TUSKS FOR DISPLAY.

THEY HELP IT DIG UP ROOTS, TOO.

HUGE HUNTER

Yangchuanosaurus is the biggest predator in Late Jurassic China. More heavily built than its North American cousin Allosaurus, it is better at steady tracking than high-speed chases. Like Allosaurus, Yangchuanosaurus boasts a massive head with powerful, bone-crunching jaws.

Yangchuanosaurus probably hunts in small packs, stalking its prey over long distances. It specializes in large sauropods, such as Mamenchisaurus, and shares the spoils with its pack mates. Yangchuanosaurus also attacks stegosaurs, such as Tuojiangosaurus, not put off by their defensive spikes and plates.

Yangchuanosaurus lives in lush valleys and woodlands.

Large, serrated teeth.

DINO DATA

**YANGCHUANOSAURUS (YANG-CHWAN-OH-SAWR-USS)
MEANING: "LIZARD FROM YONGCHUAN"**

FAMILY: METRIACANTHOSAURIDAE
TIME: LATE JURASSIC
DIET: MEAT

HEIGHT: 3.7 M (12 FT)
LENGTH: 10.8 M
(35.4 FT)
WEIGHT: 3.4 TONNES
(3.7 TONS)

Mamenchisaurus rears up in panic.

Massive, 1.1-m (3.6-ft) long skull.

FIELD NOTES

Like many theropods, Yangchuanosaurus has feathers. Perhaps the males have brighter ones during the breeding season?

SURVIVAL GUIDE:
YANGCHUANOSAURUS

Make sure Yangchuanosaurus doesn't start tracking you! Hide your prints by raking over the ground or covering them with vegetation.

SPIKED SAUROPOD

With pairs of spikes running along its neck and back, freaky-looking Amargasaurus is the punk rocker of the sauropod world. It lives in Early Cretaceous Argentina. Although it is small for a sauropod, it is still a giant among dinosaurs!

Amargasaurus grazes on tough, shrubby plants close to the ground. Its spikes may be used to defend against predators. By bending its head down, Amargasaurus can point the spikes right at any potential attacker. It might also shake its neck to make the spikes clatter—what a disturbing sound!

SAIL THEORIES

Some experts think Amargasaurus's spikes might support a pair of sails, made of webbed skin. These could help it to regulate its temperature —or perhaps the dinosaur uses them to communicate with other members of the herd.

Box-shaped snout.

Relatively small skull.

DINO SURVIVAL ESSENTIALS
FIRST-AID KIT

Make sure you know basic first-aid skills and always carry a well-stocked first-aid kit—it could make the difference between life and death out in dinosaur country!

Blunt, peg-like teeth.

For a sauropod, Amargasaurus has a relatively short neck—just 2.4 m (7.9 ft) long.

The tallest spikes are on the middle part of the neck.

DINO DATA

AMARGASAURUS (AM-AHG-OH-SAWR-USS)
MEANING: "LIZARD FROM LA AMARGA"

FAMILY: DICRAEOSAURIDAE
TIME: EARLY CRETACEOUS
DIET: PLANTS

HEIGHT: 2.4 M (7.9 FT)
LENGTH: 10 M (33 FT)
WEIGHT: 2.4 TONNES
(2.6 TONS)

RECORD BREAKERS

Sauropods are the largest dinosaurs ever—and the size record seems to be broken every time a new species is found. When Brachiosaurus was discovered in 1903, it was the largest known dinosaur. Today that record is held by a titanosaur that weighs TWICE as much as Brachiosaurus!

Brachiosaurus is 30 m (98 ft) long and lives in Jurassic North America. It eats around 120 kg (260 lb) of plant food a day. It's about as long as six family cars placed end to end.

Diplodocus measures about 33 m (108 ft), including its long, whip-like tail, and weighs around 15 tonnes (16.5 tons). Its teeth are shaped for stripping greenery off branches.

WEIGHTY MATTERS

Early dinosaur experts didn't believe that sauropods could support their own body weight on land. They thought such enormous animals must live in water, rather like today's largest animal, the blue whale.

Weighing in at around 73 tonnes (80 tons), Argentinosaurus is one of the largest dinosaurs ever. It belongs to the titanosaurs or "giant lizards" group. Just one of its vertebrae (spine bones) is almost as tall as a person! It is named after the country where it was discovered—Argentina!

FIELD NOTES

The thigh bone of the new, unnamed titanosaur is taller than a man!

This titanosaur is so new that it doesn't have a name yet! It lives in Argentina and is 40 m (131 ft) long and 20 m (65.6 ft) tall. It's an absolute monster—about 4 tonnes (4.4 tons) heavier than Argentinosaurus!

SURVIVAL GUIDE:
SAUROPOD

Sauropods eat a lot of vegetation —and create a lot of dung! Luckily, this makes a useful fuel. Collect it (holding your nose), dry it in the sun and save it for when you need to use fire to see off dangerous predators.

GIANT HUNTER

One of the largest predatory dinosaurs ever, Spinosaurus lives along swampy coastlines in Late Cretaceous North Africa. It's a specialist fish-eater, but also feeds on dinosaurs and other land prey. Its crocodilian snout is lined with large, conical teeth.

Spinosaurus's most striking feature is the big sail on its back, supported by long spines growing out of its backbone. The sail helps Spinosaurus keep its body temperature steady and is probably also used in displays directed at other spinosaurs.

FOSSIL FISH

Spinosaurus feeds by darting its head underwater and snatching up fish in its snout. One of the fish it eats is the coelacanth. People thought this primitive fish was extinct until one was found in an African lake during the 1930s.

Spinosaurus's longest spines are more than 1.65 m (5.4 ft) long.

Narrow, crocodile-like snout.

Young plesiosaur.

Strong, short arms with three-fingered hands.

Sail is supported by tall, bony spines.

DINO DATA

SPINOSAURUS (SPY-NOH-SAWR-USS)
MEANING: "SPINE LIZARD"

FAMILY: SPINOSAURIDAE
TIME: EARLY TO LATE CRETACEOUS
DIET: FISH, MEAT

HEIGHT: 6 M (20 FT)
LENGTH: 16 M (52.5 FT)
WEIGHT: 9 TONNES (9.9 TONS)

DANGER ZONE: SWAMP

Proceed through a swampy habitat with caution. It's all too easy to get stuck or lose your footing. One trick is to test the depth of dangerous-looking areas by poking a stick into the water as you go.

Muscular back legs.

Coelacanth.

HUGE CLAWS

Three massive, curved claws.

Therizinosaurus must be one of the craziest theropods ever. First of all, it mostly eats plants. Secondly, it has lethal weapons instead of hands—two trios of fearsome, slashing claws. No other animal has claws this big.

Therizinosaurus uses its massive claws to pull down tree branches and perhaps to go "fishing" in termite mounds. Killer claws also come in handy when the dinosaur needs to scare off a predator. In its Late Cretaceous Mongolian habitat, the main threat is Tarbosaurus, the Asian T. rex.

FIELD NOTES

Some members of the therizinosaur family look after their eggs until they hatch. Therizinosaurus might do this, or it might leave the young to fend for themselves.

DINO DATA

THERIZINOSAURUS (THEH-RIZ-IN-OH-SAWR-USS)
MEANING: "SCYTHE LIZARD"

FAMILY: THERIZINOSAURIDAE
TIME: LATE CRETACEOUS
DIET: PLANTS

HEIGHT: 3.7 M (12 FT)
LENGTH: 10 M (33 FT)
WEIGHT: 5 TONNES
(5.5 TONS)

Downy feathers keep Therizinosaurus warm.

Large stomach for digesting plants.

Four back toes rest on the ground (most theropods only have three).

Never hide in a high branch when Therizinosaurus is about. This dinosaur might catapult you off it while pulling down the branch to eat leaves!

Therizinosaurus's claws are a terrifying 1 m (3.3 ft) long.

SHARK TEETH

Carcharodontosaurus and Giganotosaurus are two monster theropods. Although they live on different continents, they are close cousins. They belong to a family called the shark-toothed lizards and have sharp, slicing teeth up to 20 cm (8 in) long.

SKIN QUESTIONS

Fossils cannot tell us everything we know about what dinosaurs looked like. Impressions in the rock can show if a dinosaur had scaly skin or feathers. There is no record, though, of whether dinosaurs were dull and camouflaged or showy and flamboyant.

Carcharodontosaurus is about 11 m (36 ft) long. This terrifying theropod is one of the top predators in northern Africa during the Late Cretaceous. It shares its territory with another carnivorous giant, Spinosaurus.

Carcharodontosaurus's vicious, serrated teeth look like those of the great white shark (whose Latin name is Carcharodon). They can do as much damage, too.

At 12 m (39 ft) long, Giganotosaurus is a bit bigger than Carcharodontosaurus, but has a similar physique. Often working in threes or fours, it outwits and kills Argentinosaurus and other enormous sauropods. This one's pulling flesh off an Argentinosaurus's thigh bone!

Giganotosaurus needs a strong, stocky neck to support its massive, 1.5-m (5-ft) skull. Its blade-like teeth are designed for slicing through flesh.

SURVIVAL GUIDE:
CARCHARODONTOSAURUS

Scan the sky for Ornithocheirus—if you see this scavenging pterosaur, there is probably a Carcharodontosaurus kill site nearby!

FIELD NOTES

Giganotosaurus's name means "giant southern lizard."

GIGANOTOSAURUS'S TOP SPEED IS AROUND 50 KPH (31 MPH).

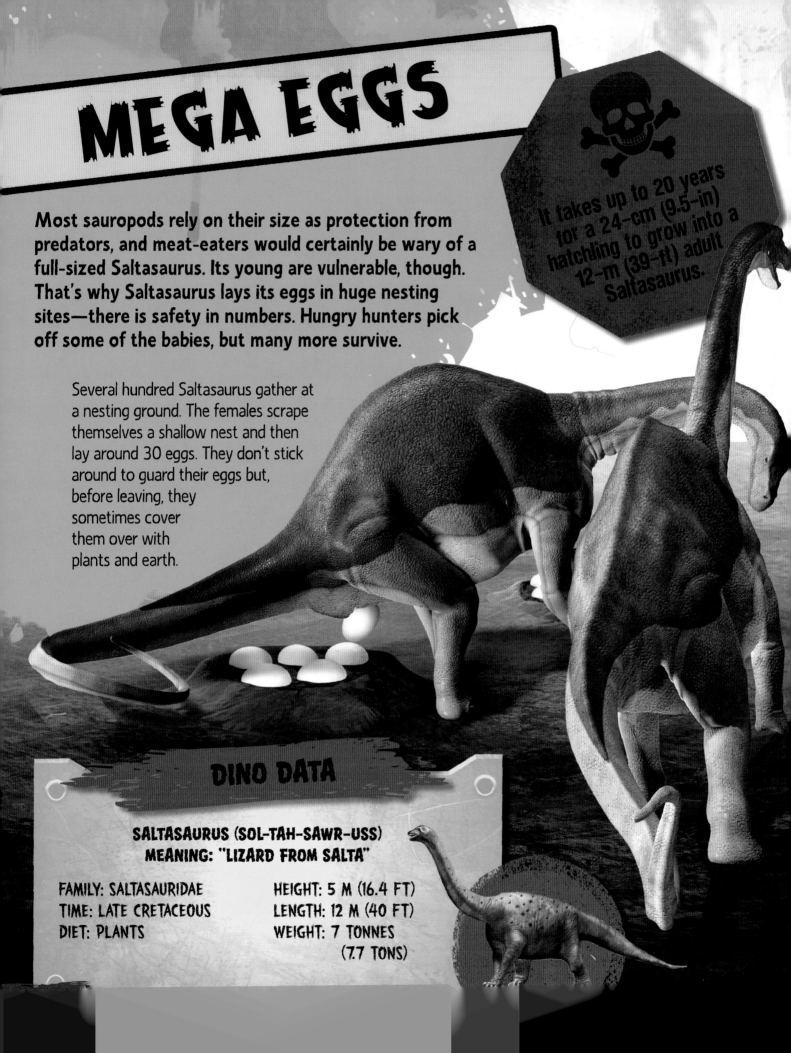

MEGA EGGS

Most sauropods rely on their size as protection from predators, and meat-eaters would certainly be wary of a full-sized Saltasaurus. Its young are vulnerable, though. That's why Saltasaurus lays its eggs in huge nesting sites—there is safety in numbers. Hungry hunters pick off some of the babies, but many more survive.

Several hundred Saltasaurus gather at a nesting ground. The females scrape themselves a shallow nest and then lay around 30 eggs. They don't stick around to guard their eggs but, before leaving, they sometimes cover them over with plants and earth.

It takes up to 20 years for a 24-cm (9.5-in) hatchling to grow into a 12-m (39-ft) adult Saltasaurus.

DINO DATA

SALTASAURUS (SOL-TAH-SAWR-USS)
MEANING: "LIZARD FROM SALTA"

FAMILY: SALTASAURIDAE
TIME: LATE CRETACEOUS
DIET: PLANTS

HEIGHT: 5 M (16.4 FT)
LENGTH: 12 M (40 FT)
WEIGHT: 7 TONNES
(7.7 TONS)

Never, ever touch a Saltasaurus egg if the mother is nearby. They can become very aggressive if they think their eggs are being stolen!

Predatory Aucasaurus lurks, hoping to snatch a hatchling.

Each egg is 12 cm (4.7 in) across—about the size of an ostrich egg.

CHAPTER FOUR: BATTLING DINOSAURS

You don't want to get in the way of the dinosaurs in this chapter. They may all be plant-eaters, but they are tough and ready for battle. Their bodies have spikes, clubs, plates, shields, and other defensive features that can inflict serious damage.

The beasts here live together in herds. They are ornithischian, or bird-hipped dinosaurs. They may not look alike from the outside, but the arrangement of their hip bones is very distinctive. Confusingly, birds are actually descended from lizard-hipped, not bird-hipped dinosaurs!

SEE PAGES 72-73

Gastonia protects itself with both spikes and plates. This 5-m (16.4-ft) long ankylosaur is from Early Cretaceous North America.

SEE PAGE 79

Styracosaurus is a large horned-face dinosaur, or ceratopsian. It inhabits North America during the Cretaceous.

SURVIVAL GUIDE: BATTLING DINOSAURS

Herd animals can stampede! Never try to run with the stampede—you'll stumble and be trampled.

EARLY ORNITHISCHIAN

Heterodontosaurus is one of the first bird-hipped dinosaurs. It is only about 1 m (3.3 ft) long and lives in South Africa during the Early Jurassic. Its name means "different-toothed lizard" and this adaptable dinosaur has three kinds of teeth: small front teeth for nipping off plant stems, longer squared-off teeth at the back of its mouth for chewing, and a pair of tusks for showing off to rivals.

This dinosaur has the typical neck frill of a ceratopsian, but no spiky horns. It is Protoceratops, an early ceratopsian from Cretaceous China.

SEE PAGE 78

SEE PAGES 80–81

Tuojiangosaurus is one of the stegosaurs, which have plates along their back and spikes at the end of their tail. It roams across China in the Late Jurassic.

Parasaurolophus is identified by its long head crest. This Late Cretaceous creature is one of the hadrosaurs (duck-billed dinosaurs).

SEE PAGE 71

KNOBBLY BEAST

Probably an ancestor to both the stegosaurs and the ankylosaurs, Scelidosaurus is one of the first shielded dinosaurs. It has rows of bony plates called scutes along its back, and pebbly bumps all over its leathery hide that stop predators biting into its skin.

Scelidosaurus is not the brightest dinosaur—compared to its body size, its brain is very small. However, it's well designed for its plant-eating life. It has a small head and beaky, slender jaw with leaf-shaped teeth. It browses on vegetation close to the ground.

Oval plates
or scutes.

Stout legs.

DINO DATA

SCELIDOSAURUS (SKELL-EYE-DOH-SAWR-USS)
MEANING: "LIMB LIZARD"

FAMILY: SCELIDOSAURIDAE
TIME: EARLY JURASSIC
DIET: PLANTS

HEIGHT: 1.5 M (5 FT)
LENGTH: 4 M (13 FT)
WEIGHT: 270 KG (595 LB)

Found in 1858, Scelidosaurus is the earliest complete dinosaur fossil.

Back legs are longer than the front ones.

SHIELDED COUSIN

Scutellosaurus is around at the same time as Scelidosaurus and is one of its relatives. It lives in North America and its name means "little-shielded lizard." Its back is covered with parallel rows of bony studs, and there are also spikes running down it.

SURVIVAL GUIDE: SCELIDOSAURUS

If a Scelidosaurus is heading your way, stand your ground and shout at the top of your voice. Hopefully, the noise will put it off and it will quickly change direction!

PLATED LIZARDS

The stegosaurs, or plated lizards, are a group of dinosaurs that have one or two rows of strange, diamond-shaped plates along their backs. The plates can be in pairs or staggered. Stegosaurs also have a thagomizer—a group of defensive tail spikes.

Stegosaurs all take their name from Stegosaurus, who ranges across North America and in Europe during the Middle Jurassic. It's the heaviest stegosaur, weighing around 4.5 tonnes (5 tons).

This is Huayangosaurus from Middle Jurassic China, the earliest known stegosaur. Its plates are organized in pairs and it has a large spike sticking out from each shoulder.

SURVIVAL GUIDE
STEGOSAURUS

Never get in the way of Stegosaurus's tail spikes! Luckily, guessing when this dinosaur will swing its tail shouldn't be too tricky—its brain is walnut-sized!

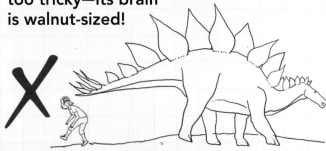

FIELD NOTES

Stegosaurs are herbivores but it's possible they eat whatever they find —not just plants but also worms, shellfish, and carrion.

Weighing in at just 1 tonne (1.1 tons), Kentrosaurus ("prickle lizard") is small for a stegosaur. It lives in Late Jurassic Africa. It defends itself by swinging its flexible, spiked tail at attackers.

PLATE PURPOSE

No one is sure what stegosaurs' plates are for. It's most likely they are used for display, but some experts think they might have also helped the dinosaurs to control their body temperature.

Tuojiangosaurus of Late Jurassic China is named after the Tuo River, where it's been found. About three-quarters the length of Stegosaurus, it weighs around 2.8 tonnes (3 tons).

Wuerhosaurus lives in China during the Early Cretaceous. It is one of the last stegosaurs. Its neck is longer than earlier stegosaurs' but its legs are shorter, so it probably specializes in eating low-growing vegetation. Its plates are rounder and flatter.

SUPER SHIELDS

Gastonia is one of the ankylosaurs, dinosaurs that have plated shields to protect themselves against predators. Gastonia certainly needs to be able to defend itself because it shares its Early Cretaceous habitat with the fearsome pack hunter, Utahraptor (see pages 40-41).

Besides its plates, Gastonia has a selection of defensive spikes —flattened ones along its sides, longer, pointier ones at its shoulders, and smaller ones along its tail, too. Unlike most ankylosaurs, it doesn't have a club-like, bumpy bone at the end of the tail for swinging at attackers. Even so, Gastonia is equipped with some formidable weaponry!

Tail lacks the typical ankylosaur tail club.

Long shoulder spikes.

DINO DATA

GASTONIA (GAS-TOE-NEE-AH)
MEANING: "FOR ROB GASTON"

FAMILY: POLACANTHIDAE
TIME: EARLY CRETACEOUS
DIET: PLANTS

HEIGHT: 3 M (10 FT)
LENGTH: 5 M (16.4 FT)
WEIGHT: 1.9 TONNES (2.1 TONS)

Triangular spikes along side.

Lack of light creates all sorts of dangers. You can stumble into swamps or off cliffs. One of Gastonia's relatives, Minmi, lives near the south pole in semi-darkness for much of the year.

Gastonia has a thick, domed skull—cushioning for when it headbutts rival males!

Domed skull with "shock-absorbers" in the bones surrounding the brain.

BEAKY BEAST

Psittacosaurus is a small, stocky plant-eater with a short, deep skull. It might seem harmless, but if you get too close, its toothless beak will make short work of your finger. As well as being able to chop through tough plant stems, it is strong enough to crack nuts!

Psittacosaurus babies "crawl" on all fours, but as they grow, their back legs lengthen. The adults are bipedal (move on two legs). One of Psittacosaurus's strangest habits is gobbling down stones. The stones sit in its gut and help mash up the unchewed plant matter there, so it can be digested.

This Psittacosaurus species has a strange, bristly tail.

SURVIVAL GUIDE:
PSITTACOSAURUS

If you're unlucky enough to brush against Psittacosaurus's tail bristles, don't move and send a friend for medical help. The bristles may contain venom. Staying still will stop it spreading through the body.

A Sinovenator pack has surrounded this Psittacosaurus.

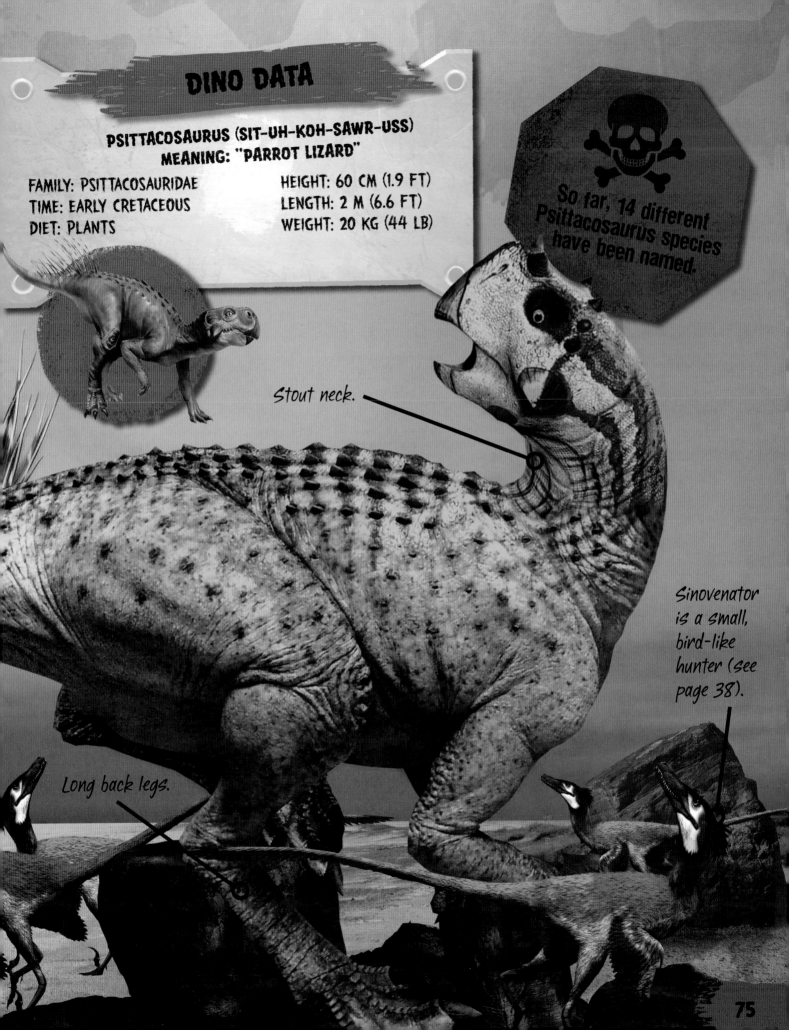

DINO DATA

PSITTACOSAURUS (SIT-UH-KOH-SAWR-USS)
MEANING: "PARROT LIZARD"

FAMILY: PSITTACOSAURIDAE
TIME: EARLY CRETACEOUS
DIET: PLANTS

HEIGHT: 60 CM (1.9 FT)
LENGTH: 2 M (6.6 FT)
WEIGHT: 20 KG (44 LB)

So far, 14 different Psittacosaurus species have been named.

Stout neck.

Long back legs.

Sinovenator is a small, bird-like hunter (see page 38).

TRIPLE TERROR

A heavyweight of the dinosaur world, Triceratops boasts three impressive horns—a shorter nose horn plus a scary pair of 1-m (3.3-ft) brow ones. Triceratops uses the brow horns to defend itself and, like stags' antlers, for showing off.

The main feature of Triceratops's enormous skull is its backward-pointing frill. This has blood vessels near the surface. By reddening or growing paler, the frill probably communicates messages to other herd members, such as warning of nearby danger or showing the dinosaur's readiness to mate.

Neck frill.

Brow horn.

Nose horn.

DINO DATA

TRICERATOPS (TRY-SERRA-TOPS)
MEANING: "THREE-HORNED FACE"

FAMILY: CERATOPSIDAE
TIME: LATE CRETACEOUS
DIET: PLANTS

HEIGHT: 3 M (10 FT)
LENGTH: 8.5 M (28 FT)
WEIGHT: 8 TONNES
(8.8 TONS)

Total length of skull is around 2 m (6.6 ft).

HIDDEN IN THE BONES

Several near-complete Triceratops skeletons have been found, as well as around 50 skulls. Some specimens have Tyrannosaurus bite marks. One even had a brow horn snapped off by T. rex!

Triceratops is one of the last dinosaurs—it dies out in the mass extinction 65 million years ago.

Beaky mouth with a few hundred teeth.

SURVIVAL GUIDE: TRICERATOPS

Avoid a charging Triceratops by running into scrubby bush. The Triceratops won't follow you there, and you'll be too intent on escape to notice any thorns!

HORNED HORRORS

Psittacosaurus and Triceratops belong to a group of dinosaurs called the ceratopsians, or horned-face lizards. Psittacosaurus is one of the more primitive members, with just a beaked face. Later ones, including Triceratops and most of the dinosaurs here, have horns and showy neck frills.

Sheep-sized Protoceratops is one of the earlier ceratopsians. It digs its nest with its spade-like front claws and lays about 15 eggs at a time.

FIELD NOTES

Protoceratops is one of the least impressive ceratopsians—it doesn't really have any horns and its frill is very modest!

Zuniceratops is the missing link between the earliest ceratopsians and later ones. It lacks a nose horn, but does have a couple of brow horns and a frill. It is about 3.25 m (10.7 ft) long.

Weighing in at nearly 3 tonnes (3.3 tons), Styracosaurus ("spiked lizard") is one of the largest—and spikiest!—ceratopsians. The six biggest horns on its neck frill are each more than 50 cm (20 in) long. It has cheek horns, too.

At around 6 m (20 ft) long, Centrosaurus is another of the larger ceratopsians. Its name means "pointed lizard" and refers to the spiky hornlets (little horns) edging its neck frill.

Chasmosaurus's name means "wide opening lizard." This dinosaur has two huge holes in its frill bone, which are covered over by skin. The frill is massive, but not very strong.

SURVIVAL GUIDE: CERATOPSIAN

If a small herd of ceratopsians ambles your way, don't panic! They're probably just curious. Walk on calmly. Don't make any sudden, jerky movements that could trigger a stampede.

LOUD SPEAKER

Twice as tall as a man, Parasaurolophus has a huge, backward-pointing crest on top of its head. The hollow crest helps to turn the dinosaur's everyday calls into deafening blasts of noise. Even though this animal is a gentle plant-eater, it can do your ears serious damage!

Parasaurolophus is one of the hadrosaurs, or duck-billed dinosaurs. Some hadrosaurs have solid crests. Others, like Parasaurolophus, have hollow ones. Parasaurolophus's crest probably has another purpose, too. It can soak up the sun's heat during the day, and then use that energy to keep the dinosaur warm at night.

Grazes on all fours, but runs on two legs for short bursts.

THE BIGGEST HADROSAUR IS PROBABLY 15-M (49-FT) LONG SHANTUNGOSAURUS.

DINO SURVIVAL ESSENTIALS
EAR PLUGS

If you have to set up camp near a noisy Parasaurolophus herd, you'll need ear plugs to block out the noise. Be careful, though. You won't be able to hear any approaching predators, either!

Narrow beak for snipping off vegetation.

Head crest.

Powerful shoulder muscles.

Slender neck.

DINO DATA

PARASAUROLOPHUS (PARA-SAW-ROLL-UH-FUSS)
MEANING: "NEAR-CRESTED LIZARD"

FAMILY: DROMAEOSAURIDAE   HEIGHT: 3.6 M (11 FT)
TIME: LATE CRETACEOUS   LENGTH: 11 M (36 FT)
DIET: PLANTS   WEIGHT: 2.5 TONNES (2.8 TONS)

THICK-HEADED LIZARD

Pachycephalosaurus's strangely domed skull looks as though it could amplify sound — but it's not hollow like Parasaurolophus's. Pachycephalosaurus is one of the bone-headed dinosaurs and it's a champion headbutter!

FIERCE MOTHER

Never come between a Maiasaura and its eggs or hatchlings. This dinosaur's name means "good mother lizard"—though of course, the species includes males as well as females! Maiasaura is a sociable creature, living together in massive herds of up to 10,000 individuals.

Maiasaura likes company when raising its young, so it nests in colonies. The nests are tightly packed, with less than an adult's body length between each one. A nest contains between 15 and 40 eggs. When the babies hatch, the parents bring them food.

DINO DATA

MAIASAURA (MAY-A-SAWR-A)
MEANING: "GOOD MOTHER LIZARD"

FAMILY: HADROSAURIDAE
TIME: LATE CRETACEOUS
DIET: PLANTS

HEIGHT: 2.3 M (7.5 FT)
LENGTH: 9 M (29.5 FT)
WEIGHT: 2 TONNES
(2.2 TONS)

Maiasaura was the first dinosaur in space! Its fossils took a journey on NASA's space shuttle in 1985.

Small, solid crest in front of eyes.

Hold your nose if you get caught up in a Maiasaura nesting colony—the eggs are incubated with rotting vegetation.

Horny beak.

Maiasaura egg.

Crater-shaped nest.

FIELD NOTES

Maiasaura hatchlings don't have a crest—the crest grows as the dinosaurs mature.

Hatchling

CLUB ATTACK

Ankylosaurus is a gigantic beast, the largest of the shielded dinosaurs. Every part of its thick, leathery skin (except its belly) is studded with hundreds of bite-proof bony plates. However, Ankylosaurus's most powerful defensive weapon is its big, bone-shattering tail club.

Ankylosaurus has enough mobility in its 2-m (6.6-ft) tail to swing it at great force, and that's when the huge club at the end does its damage. It's how Ankylosaurus defends itself from hunters. This tank of a dinosaur also has four head spikes to protect the area around its eyes.

TUBE MYSTERY

Ankylosaurus's snout bulges out at the sides because the bone contains a network of air passages. No one is sure what the passages are for—perhaps they amplify noises that the dinosaur makes.

Ankylosaurus is capable of breaking one of T. rex's legs with its tail club!

SURVIVAL GUIDE: ANKYLOSAURUS

Ankylosaurus's tail club is about level with a person's head. The best way to avoid being concussed is to crouch low or climb high!

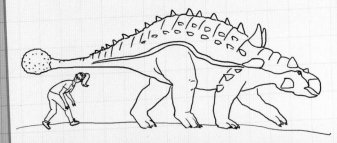

84

DINO DATA

ANKYLOSAURUS (ANK-ILL-OH-SAWR-USS)
MEANING: "FUSED LIZARD"

FAMILY: ANKYLOSAURIDAE
TIME: LATE CRETACEOUS
DIET: PLANTS

HEIGHT: 1.7 M (5.6 FT)
LENGTH: 6.25 M (20.5 FT)
WEIGHT: 6 TONNES (6.6 TONS)

Bony tail club.

Skull houses very small brain.

Head spike.

Beaky mouth is toothless at the front, with small teeth at the sides.

CHAPTER FIVE: FLYING MONSTERS

While dinosaurs dominate the land, other reptiles rule the air. These are the pterosaurs, or "winged lizards." Leathery wings outstretched, they swoop and dive across seas and along coastlines, snatching up fish or landing to tuck into carrion.

Pterosaurs come in all sizes. The smallest has a wingspan of just 2.5 cm (1 in), while larger species are like light aircraft (and still hold the record for being the biggest flying animals ever). Pterosaurs first appear around 200 million years ago in the Late Triassic, but their heyday is the Late Jurassic.

SEE PAGES 88-89

The Early Jurassic pterosaur Dimorphodon has been spotted in sites as far apart as Mexico and England.

SEE PAGES 96-97

The sky doesn't belong only to pterosaurs. This cute creature with sharp teeth is Volaticotherium, a flying mammal.

In terms of size, the most monstrous pterosaur is South America's Tropeognathus. Its whopping wingspan is wider than 8 m (27 ft).

The first pterosaurs are probably all insectivores (insect-eaters).

SEE PAGES 98-99

PTEROSAURS AND BIRDS

Pterosaurs don't evolve into birds —dinosaurs do! However, some pterosaurs must share the skies with the first birds, such as Archaeopteryx (below) who lives in the Late Jurassic.

SURVIVAL GUIDE: FLYING MONSTERS

Take cover! A pterosaur is unlikely to spot you hiding in the undergrowth, so long as you don't move a muscle.

SEE PAGES 102–103

Medium-sized Eudimorphodon is one of the earliest pterosaurs. Its wingspan is around 1 m (3.3 ft) and it lives in the Late Triassic.

With a wingspan of 6 m (20 ft), Pteranodon is one of the larger pterosaurs. It is also one of the last—it lives in the Late Cretaceous.

SEE PAGE 101

PTEROSAURS WERE THE FIRST LARGE ANIMALS TO MASTER THE ART OF FLYING.

INSECTS WERE THE FIRST FLIERS, THOUGH.

DEADLY DIMORPHODON

At around 1 m (3.3 ft) long, Dimorphodon is one of the medium-sized pterosaurs—but that's about the only average thing about it. This freaky flier has a huge, puffin-like head and two different kinds of teeth in its jaws.

Dimorphodon isn't a graceful glider. Its short wings mean that it moves through the air in jerky little bursts. However, this pterosaur is good at running. It chases after insects, gobbles up other small prey, such as lizards, and sometimes scoops up fish.

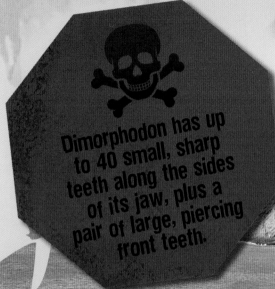

Dimorphodon has up to 40 small, sharp teeth along the sides of its jaw, plus a pair of large, piercing front teeth.

Puffin-like head.

DIMORPHODON DISCOVERY

Mary Anning was a 19th-century fossil hunter who lived in Lyme Regis, Dorset, England. She found many important fossils, including the first-ever Dimorphodon in 1828.

Clifftop home.

BEASTLY DATA

DIMORPHODON (DIE-MORE-FOE-DON)
MEANING: "TWO TEETH SHAPES"

FAMILY: DIMORPHODONTIDAE
TIME: EARLY JURASSIC
DIET: INSECTS, MEAT, FISH

LENGTH: 1 M (3.3 FT)
WINGSPAN: 1.4 M (4.6 FT)
WEIGHT: 2.3 KG (5 LB)

SURVIVAL GUIDE:
DIMORPHODON

If a Dimorphodon flies at you, fall to the ground, roll into a ball and play dead.

Muscular back legs.

"Chick."

Relatively short wings.

Grasping claws.

TOOTHY TERROR

Long-tailed pterosaur Rhamphorhynchus flies low over lakes and stretches of sea, dipping its curved jaw into the water to snatch fishy prey. Its pointy beak contains 34 sharp little teeth, although the very tip is toothless. Rhamphorhynchus hunts insects, too.

Rhamphorhynchus belongs to the rhamphorhynchoids—the group of pterosaurs with long tails. The other group of pterosaurs is the pterodactyls. Rhamphorhynchus's tail has a diamond-shaped flap at the end that helps the pterosaur steer, like a rudder.

SURVIVAL GUIDE: RHAMPHORHYNCHUS

Make yourself look big and scary if you spot a Rhamphorhynchus flying your way. Wave your arms over your head.

Needle-like teeth.

It's possible that Rhamphorhynchus has a pouched, pelican-like throat for scooping up fish.

BEASTLY DATA

RHAMPHORHYNCHUS (RAM-FOE-RINK-USS)
MEANING: "BEAK SNOUT"

FAMILY: RHAMPHORHYNCHIDAE
TIME: JURASSIC
DIET: INSECTS, FISH

LENGTH: 1.3 M (4 FT)
WINGSPAN: 1.8 M (6 FT)
WEIGHT: 3.4 KG (7.5 LB)

Diamond-shaped tail rudder.

Long tail.

RHAMPHORHYNCHUS'S TEETH CLOSE TO FORM A "CAGE."

SLIPPERY FISH JUST CANNOT ESCAPE!

FAMED PTEROSAUR

For a while, people mistakenly called all pterosaurs "pterodactyls," after Pterodactylus, the first pterosaur fossil to be discovered. But Pterodactylus is just one of many weird and wonderful pterosaurs, all with their own ways of competing for food and territory.

Pterodactylus, the first known pterosaur, lives in Late Jurassic Germany. It's relatively small, with a wingspan of around 1 m (3.3 ft).

This flock of Anhanguera is catching fish. The beaks of these large South American pterosaurs have spoon-shaped tips that make it easier to scoop up fish.

EARLY EXPERTS MISTOOK PTERODACTYLUS'S WINGS FOR FLIPPERS.

THEY THOUGHT IT WAS A WEIRD MARINE AMPHIBIAN!

PTEROSAUR SKIN

Pterosaurs don't have feathers—they have scaly, reptilian skin. However, some species have a covering of hair-like filaments, called pycnofibers. The small Late Jurassic pterosaur called Sordes has these.

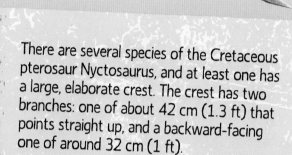

There are several species of the Cretaceous pterosaur Nyctosaurus, and at least one has a large, elaborate crest. The crest has two branches: one of about 42 cm (1.3 ft) that points straight up, and a backward-facing one of around 32 cm (1 ft).

Ctenochasma's name means "comb jaw." This Late Jurassic pterosaur's jaw is lined with long, super-thin teeth, packed so tightly together they look like bristles. They allow Ctenochasma to sieve the water for snacks.

SURVIVAL GUIDE:
PTEROSAUR

Always watch out near cliffs! As well as facing rockfalls and surprising tides, you might be attacked by pterosaurs if you get too close to their nests.

ANCIENT WING

Raven-sized Archaeopteryx is sometimes called the first bird, but it shares more characteristics with dromaeosaurs than modern birds. It has killer claws, a long tail, and a jaw packed with sharp teeth. It's sometimes called the "missing link"!

Archaeopteryx isn't a tree dweller. It hunts at ground level, seizing insects and small animals in its jaws. It's a good bet that Archaeopteryx can fly, thanks to its broad, rounded wings and long feathered tail, but experts aren't sure if it does so by flapping or gliding.

Archaeopteryx lives on islands formed by coral reefs and surrounded by shallow lagoons.

DANGER ZONE: LAGOON

Don't try and drink water from lagoons —cut off from the sea by reefs, they often become super-salty as their water evaporates in the hot Jurassic sun. Beware of falling in, too. The water's shallow, and if you sink into the soft mud on the bottom, you're doomed!

Cone-shaped teeth in pointed snout.

Feathered upper legs.

Four-toed feet.

Tail feathers.

Three-fingered claws for pinning down larger prey.

DINO DATA

ARCHAEOPTERYX (ARK-EE-OP-TEAR-IKS)
MEANING: "ANCIENT WING"

FAMILY: ARCHAEOPTERYGIDAE
TIME: LATE JURASSIC
DIET: PLANTS, INSECTS, MEAT

LENGTH: 30 CM (1 FT)
WINGSPAN: 50 CM (20 IN)
WEIGHT: 1 KG (2.2 LB)

MAMMAL GLIDER

Reptiles are not the only animals taking to the skies. Around the Middle Jurassic, a rat-sized mammal called Volaticotherium is gliding through China's forests. Its "wing," or gliding membrane, is a flap of skin stretched between its four limbs and its tail.

Volaticotherium's long tail acts as a rudder, helping it to steer. Its hands and feet have large claws that grip tree bark as the animal clambers and climbs. This little beast feasts on insects. Its jaw is packed with specialized teeth: incisors for cutting, canines for stabbing, and premolars and molars for grinding.

Fur-covered gliding membrane.

Long tail for steering.

Volaticotherium is the earliest known gliding mammal.

Large claws

Sharp, hooked teeth

SURVIVAL GUIDE: VOLATICOTHERIUM

Volaticotherium is small, but it has a nasty bite. Scare it off by singing or shouting loudly. If that fails, frighten it with fire!

MODERN GLIDERS

The sugar glider is a type of possum, and it is one of many modern-day animals that glide. Others include flying frogs, flying Draco lizards, and flying squirrels. Gliding is a great way to move from tree to tree because it doesn't use up much energy.

BEASTLY DATA

VOLATICOTHERIUM (VOL-AT-IK-OH-THEER-EE-UM)
MEANING: "GLIDING BEAST"

FAMILY: TRICONODONTIDAE
TIME: MIDDLE JURASSIC TO EARLY CRETACEOUS
DIET: INSECTS

LENGTH: 20 CM (8 IN)
WINGSPAN: 10 CM (4 IN)
WEIGHT: 200 G (7 OZ)

SKY GIANT

The prize for largest pterosaur must go to Tropeognathus. Its wingspan is as long as a school minibus! Found just off the coast of South America, this big beast dips its bumpy beak into the water to grab fish, squid, and other sea creatures.

Tropeognathus is named for the keel-shaped crests on its snout and lower jaw (a keel is the fin on the underside of a boat that helps keep it steady in the water). The curved shape of the crests helps Tropeognathus push its mouth into the water more efficiently.

Tropeognathus has impressive fangs at the front of its jaw.

Males probably have showier beak crests.

Jaw houses strong, conical teeth.

Enormous wing finger.

TROPEOGNATHUS (TROP-EE-OH-NAY-THUS)
MEANING: "KEEL JAW"

FAMILY: ORNITHOCHEIRIDAE
TIME: CRETACEOUS
DIET: FISH, SEA CREATURES

LENGTH: 6 M (20 FT)
WINGSPAN: 8.2 M (27 FT)
WEIGHT: 13 KG (27 LB)

Massive wingspan.

TROPEOGNATHUS WAS MISTAKEN FOR ORNITHOCHEIRUS AT FIRST.

DINO SURVIVAL ESSENTIALS

SUNGLASSES

You'll want to wear a pair of sunglasses when you're scanning the skies for Tropeognathus. It could be very dangerous if you became dazzled for even a moment!

STRANGE JAWS

Pterosaurs are equipped with all sorts of bizarre jaws, whether they're long and thin, lined with bristles, or pointy, like tweezers. Each jaw type gives its owner the advantage when it comes to hunting and eating its preferred food.

With a 7-m (23-ft) wingspan, Moganopterus is one of the largest known pterosaurs. Its long, sword-like jaw is named after **Mo** Ye and her husband **Gan** Jiang, a pair of swordsmiths in Chinese mythology.

Pterodaustro's 30-cm (1-ft) long skull has impressive, curved jaws. Hundreds of bristle-like teeth in its lower jaw strain shrimp and other invertebrates from the water.

FIELD NOTES

Moganopterus has the largest skull of any toothed pterosaur.

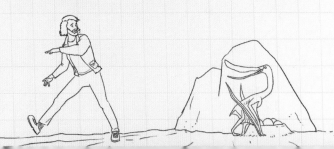

Dsungaripterus uses the upturned tip of its tweezer-like jaw to prise shellfish off rocks or winkle worms from the sand. It lives along the shorelines of Early Cretaceous China.

Eudimorphodon wins the prize for toothiest pterosaur. It has more than 100 teeth packed into its 6-cm (2.4-in) jaw—longer fangs at the front and masses of small, pointy teeth filling the rest.

PREHISTORIC FLAMINGO

Modern flamingoes use a similar feeding method to Pterodaustro—they filter-feed by pushing water through the bristles in their lower beak. Perhaps Pterodaustro's diet affects its appearance like the flamingo's does—the bird is pink because of pigments in the shrimp and algae that it eats.

Jeholopterus may be a vampire pterosaur! Some scientists think that it uses its long fangs to pierce tough dino skin, and then sucks out blood. All the while, Jeholopterus clings to its victim's skin with its super-sharp claws.

CRESTED MONSTER

Pteranodon is one of the larger pterosaurs. Supported on powerful wings, Pteranodon dive-bombs into the sea to snatch fish and other prey, which it gulps down whole. Its 1.2-m (4-ft) long, beaky snout is sharp and curved for breaking through the waves.

As well as a snout longer than its own body, Pteranodon boasts a striking, backward-pointing head crest. The crest is for display—bigger, more brightly patterned ones are more impressive, and more likely to attract a mate.

RIVAL CREST

Tapejara is only small, but this Brazilian pterosaur's crest is almost as impressive as Pteranodon's! Busy day and night, Tapejara uses its short, downturned snout to chomp on fish, carrion, and possibly fruit, too.

BEASTLY DATA

PTERANODON (TEH-RAN-OH-DON)
MEANING: "TOOTHLESS WING"

FAMILY: PTERANODONTIDAE
TIME: LATE CRETACEOUS
DIET: FISH, SEA CREATURES

LENGTH: 1.8 M (6 FT)
WINGSPAN: 6 M (20 FT)
WEIGHT: 25 KG (55 LB)

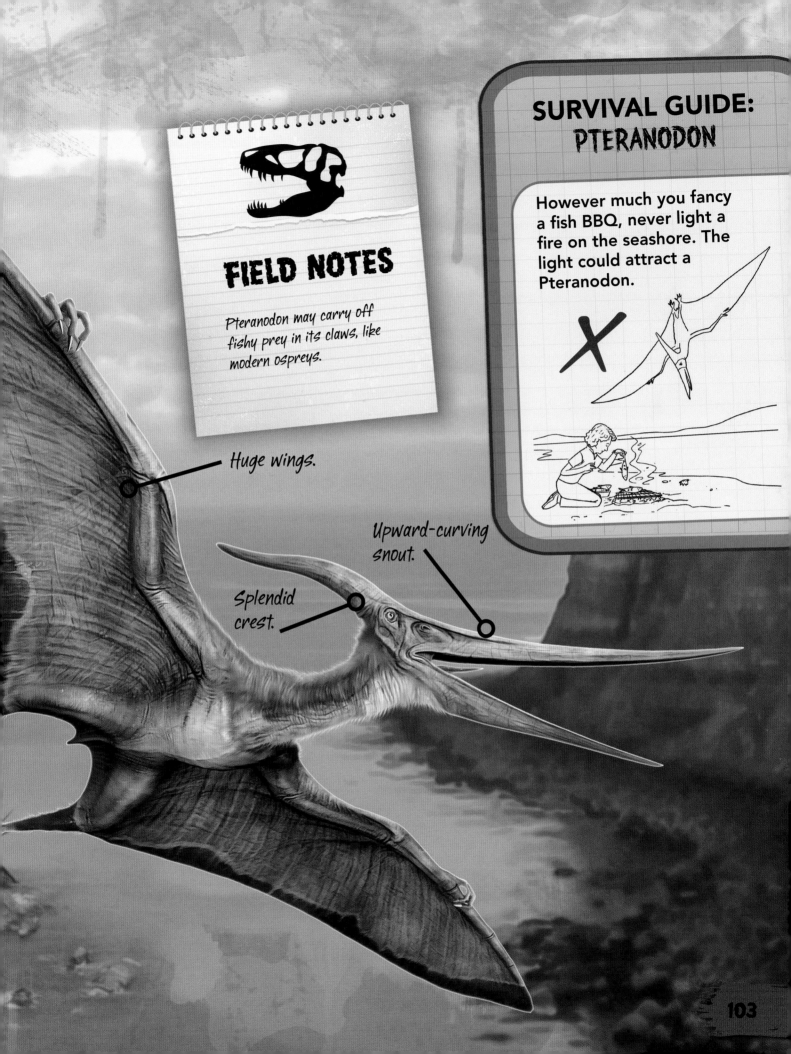

FIELD NOTES

Pteranodon may carry off fishy prey in its claws, like modern ospreys.

SURVIVAL GUIDE: PTERANODON

However much you fancy a fish BBQ, never light a fire on the seashore. The light could attract a Pteranodon.

Huge wings.

Upward-curving snout.

Splendid crest.

KING OF THE SKIES

With its 11-m (36-ft) wingspan, Quetzalcoatlus is the largest flying animal of all time. It lives right at the end of the dinosaur age. It is toothless, but equipped with a truly terrifying, stork-like snout. This pterosaur is powerful enough to prey on smaller dinosaurs.

Quetzalcoatlus spends a lot of its time inland, on the lookout for carrion to scavenge or injured dinosaurs to attack. On its four limbs, it's about as tall as a giraffe. Its muscular legs allow it to chase prey and also to launch itself skyward in a vertical take-off.

Quetzalcoatlus is named after the Aztec serpent god, Quetzalcoatl (who had to be kept happy with human sacrifices)...

BEASTLY DATA

QUETZALCOATLUS (KWET-ZAL-CO-AT-LUSS)
MEANING: "LIKE THE GOD QUETZALCOATL"

FAMILY: AZHDARCHIDAE

TIME: LATE CRETACEOUS

DIET: FISH, SHELLFISH, MEAT

HEIGHT: 4.9 M (16 FT)

WINGSPAN: 11 M (36 FT)

WEIGHT: 225 KG (496 LB)

Skull crest
for display.

A meteorite is a lump of space rock that
crashes to Earth. A large one can throw up
enough dust to block out the sun for months.
That is what happened 65 million years ago.
Experts think a meteorite impact was
responsible for pterosaurs (and
dinosaurs and many other
animals) dying out.

Long neck.

Long wings.

Quetzalcoatlus
hunts small
dinosaurs.

GIANT GLIDER

Queztalcoatlus does not waste
energy flapping its huge wings. Most
of the time, it uses warm air currents
(thermals) to stay aloft. It can glide
along for distances of around
16,000 km (9,940 miles).

CHAPTER SIX: SEA MONSTERS

SEE PAGES 122-123

Prehistoric oceans have their own horrors, including some fearsome predators. Many of these are giant versions of familiar sea creatures, including jellyfish, squid, turtles, and sharks. There are also some monstrous reptiles that don't resemble ANYTHING we know today!

The plesiosaurs are a huge family of Mesozoic marine reptiles that have flippers for limbs. Some have freakily long necks. The ichythosaurs or "fish lizards" look like dolphins from a horror film, with long, pointy jaws packed with teeth. In shallower waters, you'll also find predatory dinosaurs on the lookout for a meal.

Suchomimus is a spinosaur of the Early Cretaceous. It does most of its hunting in the water, snapping up fish in its long, narrow jaws.

Cameroceras, a monstrous mollusk, lives 465 mya, before dinosaur times. At least 6 m (20 ft) long, it has a hard shell to protect its body and grabs prey in its squid-like tentacles.

The crocodilian Dakosaurus first appears in the Late Jurassic. No one is sure if this fearsome predator spends all its life at sea, or comes ashore to breed.

SEE PAGES 110-111

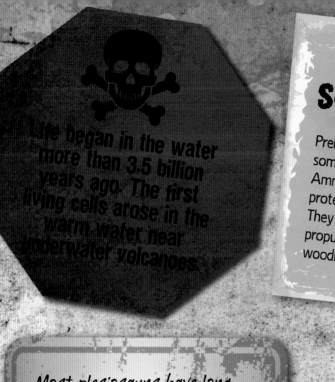

Life began in the water more than 3.5 billion years ago. The first living cells arose in the warm water near underwater volcanoes.

SHELLED SCAVENGERS

Prehistoric seas are home to some strange, shelled creatures. Ammonites have spiral shells protecting their soft bodies. They move along like squid, by jet propulsion. Trilobites are like gigantic woodlice, scavenging on the seabed.

Trilobite

Ammonite

Most plesiosaurs have long necks—at 7 m (23 ft) long, Albertonectes' is one of the most impressive! This beast cruises through Late Cretaceous seas.

SEE PAGE 113

SEE PAGE 117

Pliosaurs are short-necked plesiosaurs. Peloneustes here is one of the shortest, at around 3 m (10 ft) long. Some species grow to four times that!

SURVIVAL GUIDE: SEA MONSTERS

The best way to survive these beasts is to avoid the water altogether. If you must get in, make sure you're a good swimmer. Breathe deeply, stay calm, and keep your wits about you.

SQUID KILLER

Ichthyosaurs are fast, dolphin-like hunters. Shonisaurus is one of the earliest and also one of the biggest, measuring a gargantuan 15 m (49 ft) long. Its monstrous size means that Shonisaurus swims along at a slower pace than most of its ichthosaur relatives.

Shonisaurus's size is an advantage when it comes to pursuing its target prey. This ichthyosaur specializes in hunting squid. Its large body can take in deeper breaths so it is able to spend longer hunting in the deep. Ichthyosaurs do not have gills, so they have to come up for air.

Ichthyosaurs give birth in the water to live babies.

Lacks dorsal fin (unlike most ichthyosaurs).

Flippers are all roughly the same size.

Long-distance swimmers sometimes rub their bodies with goose fat to stay warm. Don't be tempted to do that—it will make you smell irrestistibly delicious to ichthyosaurs such as Shonisaurus!

SWORD NOSE

The ichthyosaur Excalibosaurus is named after King Arthur's legendary sword. It has the same hunting technique as modern swordfish. It slashes at fish with its elongated, sword-like upper jaw, injuring them so they cannot swim away.

Massive body.

Fish-like tail fluke.

BEASTLY DATA

SHONISAURUS (SHOW-NEE-SORE-USS)
MEANING: "LIZARD FROM THE SHOSHONE MOUNTAINS"

FAMILY: SHASTASAURIDAE
TIME: TRIASSIC
DIET: FISH, SQUID

LENGTH: 15 M (49 FT)
WEIGHT: 35 TONNES
(38.6 TONS)

DANGEROUS DAKO

Deadly Dakosaurus is an ancient sea crocodile. It's better adapted to life at sea than most crocs, with streamlined flippers instead of short legs, and a shark-like tail fin. These features make it formidable in the water, but awkward on land.

Dakosaurus preys on large fish and other marine reptiles, including ichthyosaurs. Dako means "biter" and this crocodile certainly has super-strong jaws. Like a killer whale, it uses its large, sharp teeth to take murderous chunks from its prey, gradually weakening it through blood loss.

Dakosaurus is nicknamed "Godzilla" because of its head shape.

Tail fin.

Flipper.

Ichthyosaur prey.

Serrated teeth.

SURVIVAL GUIDE: DAKOSAURUS

Never ever splash about when you're in the water —it's a sure way to attract a hungry predator.

BEASTLY DATA

DAKOSAURUS (DAK-OH-SORE-USS)
MEANING: "BITER LIZARD"

FAMILY: METRIORHYNCHIDAE
TIME: LATE JURASSIC,
   EARLY CRETACEOUS

DIET: FISH, MEAT
LENGTH: 5 M (16.4 FT)
WEIGHT: 900 KG (1 TON)

PADDLING PREDATORS

The plesiosaurs are marine reptiles that appear in the Late Triassic and stick around until the end of the Cretaceous. They have small heads, often on long necks, and feed on fish and squid. Some are absolutely enormous! The family also includes the pliosaurs (see pages 114-117).

The plesiosaurs are all named after 3.5-m (11.5-ft) long Plesiosaurus. It has a 1.5-m (4.9-ft) neck for reaching after fishy prey, and stiff flippers for paddling through the water.

Among the plesiosaurs, the neck champions are the elasmosaurs or "ribbon lizards." Half of Elasmosaurus's 14-m (46-ft) body length is neck.

SURVIVAL GUIDE: PLESIOSAUR

If you're being pursued by a plesiosaur, pull off some of your clothes. They'll distract the plesiosaur—and you'll be able to swim faster without soggy clothes dragging you down.

FIELD NOTES

The many vertebrae in a plesiosaur's neck let it sway from side to side in the water.

Like all the elasmosaurs, Albertonectes has a cunning hunting method. It sneaks up on shoals of fish from below, then lets its head spring up like a jack-in-the-box to gulp huge mouthfuls of the unsuspecting prey.

Dolichorhynchops is one of the shorter-necked plesiosaurs, with long, thin teeth for spearing fish. This 3-m (9.8-ft) long hunter is preyed upon by larger marine reptiles, such as mosasaurs (see pages 118-119).

GASTROLITHS

Plesiosaurs often gobble up stones. Known as gastroliths, these help to mash up food that has been swallowed whole, so that it is easier for the body to absorb. The stones might also work like ballast on a ship, helping the animals stay steady in the water.

Kaiwhekea is one of the last plesiosaurs. It is 7-m (23-ft) long and its name means "squid eater". Its jaw is packed with small teeth for biting into slippery prey.

SOME EXPERTS THINK THAT PLESIOSAURS' LONG NECKS HOUSE SPECIAL ELECTRO SENSORS. THESE CAN DETECT APPROACHING PREY.

BIG BITER

Liopleurodon is a top hunter of the Middle Jurassic. It's one of the pliosaurs—a particular group of plesiosaurs that have shorter necks and larger heads. Liopleurodon is a pursuit predator. Its paddle-like limbs drive it through the water after fish, squid, and ichthyosaurs.

Liopleurodon has speed on its side. Once it catches up with its prey, its next fearsome feature comes into play. Its biting strength is awesome—stronger than T. rex's! Its jaws are up to 1.5 m (5 ft) long, studded with cone-shaped teeth.

Powerful paddles allow super-fast acceleration.

Streamlined body.

Short neck.

DINO SURVIVAL ESSENTIALS

LIFE JACKET

A life jacket is an essential bit of kit if you are exploring watery environments. It will keep you afloat in treacherous waters, even when you don't have the strength to swim.

BEASTLY DATA

LIOPLEURODON (LIE-OH-PLOOR-OH-DON)
MEANING: "SMOOTH-SIDED TEETH"

FAMILY: PLIOSAURIDAE
TIME: MIDDLE JURASSIC
DIET: FISH, MEAT

LENGTH: 7 M (23 FT)
WEIGHT: 2.3 TONNES
(2.5 TONS)

SENSE OF SMELL

Most marine reptiles use their nostrils just for breathing. Liopleurodon is different. Its nostrils are lower on its head, and can probably pick up scents in the water—such as the tantalizing smell of blood!

Large head.

Liopleurodon's bite is powerful enough to cut a car in half!

FEARSOME FAMILY

This terrifying gallery is made up of powerful pliosaurs. Found all over the world, these ocean-living carnivores are known for their amazing swimming speed, crocodilian teeth and super-strong bite. They hunt fish, including sharks, as well as other marine reptiles.

At around 10 m (33 m) long, Kronosaurus is one of the largest pliosaur species. It lives in the Early Cretaceous and feeds on turtles and plesiosaurs.

MUSCLE POWER

All pliosaurs are fast swimmers, but Macroplata is especially powerful. Its relatively big shoulder bones support extra large muscles for the front flippers—the ones that do most of the pulling through the water.

Macroplata is one of the shorter pliosaurs, just over double the length of a person at around 4.5 m (14.8 ft). It also has a longer neck than other pliosaurs. It hunts at high speeds, chasing shoals of fish.

If you must swim in pliosaur-infested waters, carry an old turtle shell as a shield. A pliosaur can easily bite through the shell, but at least that will keep it busy while you concentrate on getting out of the water.

FIELD NOTES

Many pliosaurs' stomachs contain dinosaur bones. Pliosaurs don't come ashore, so the bones must be from corpses washed into the water.

In spite of its relatively small size—it's just 3 m (10 ft) long—Peloneustes is strong enough to tackle large prey. It has a taste for ammonites, even though their hard shells make its teeth go blunt.

All pliosaurs are named after the first one that was discovered—Pliosaurus. This Jurassic beast is about 10 m (33 ft) long, though one fearsome and mysterious Pliosaurus species, nicknamed Predator X, is nearer 13 m (48 ft). Its skull alone measures about 2 m (6.6 ft)!

SNAPPY EATER

Sleek and vicious, mosasaurs are the top marine predators in the Late Cretaceous. Some are just 1 m (3.3 ft) long, but the monster ones, such as Mosasaurus, dwarf everything else in the sea. Mosasaurus hunts fish, turtles, smaller mosasaurs, plesiosaurs, and ichthyosaurs.

Mosasaurus's technique for catching marine reptiles is stealth—it lurks at the surface and ambushes prey that is short of breath and coming up for air. Mosasaurus also scavenges the corpses of birds, dinosaurs, and pterosaurs that have been swept into the sea.

Mosaurus doesn't come ashore even to lay eggs—instead, it gives birth to live young out at sea.

Sturdy, barrel-like body.

BEASTLY DATA

MOSASAURUS (MOE-ZA-SORE-USS)
MEANING: "MEUSE RIVER LIZARD"

FAMILY: MOSASAURIDAE
TIME: LATE CRETACEOUS
DIET: FISH, MEAT

LENGTH: 18 M (59 FT)
WEIGHT: 5 TONNES
(5.5 TONS)

Smooth skin with tiny scales.

Darker top is hard to spot against the ocean deep.

FIELD NOTES

Mosasaurus's jaw is double-hinged like a snake's so it can open really wide, and gulp down prey whole.

Lighter underside is hard to spot against the sunlit surface.

SURVIVAL GUIDE:
MOSASAURUS

Never float about at the surface—to a mosasaur, you'll look like turtle prey.

SUPER SHARK

Sharks are a menace in prehistoric times. The largest one ever to prowl the seas is monstrous Megalodon, which lives 16 to 1.6 mya, long after the great marine reptiles of the Mesozoic die out. This deadly hunter is a whopping 18 m (59 ft) long and weighs up to 60 tonnes (66 tons).

Megalodon's formidable jaw is almost 2.7 m (9 ft tall)—an adult human can stand in there with plenty of room to spare. It is packed with rows of triangular, serrated teeth. Like other shark species, Megalodon is constantly losing teeth, but new ones move forwards to take their place. Megalodon's target prey—whales—don't stand a chance!

Massive, gaping jaw.

Gills.

BEASTLY DATA

MEGALODON (MEG-AH-LOW-DON)
MEANING: "BIG TOOTH"

FAMILY: LAMNIDAE

TIME: 16–1.6 MYA (NEOGENE)

DIET: FISH, MEAT

LENGTH: 18 M (59 FT)

WEIGHT: 60 TONNES (66 TONS)

PROTO SHARK

Hybodus is a primitive shark around during the dinosaur age. This 2-m (6.6-ft) long predator is not at all picky—it will eat anything. Unlike later sharks, it has two dorsal (back) fins instead of one, so it can steer through the water with pinpoint accuracy.

Dorsal fin for steering.

Streamlined body.

SURVIVAL GUIDE: MEGALODON

Sharks have an amazing sense of smell. Never enter the water if you have an open wound as Megalodon can sniff out blood from around 0.5 km (0.3 miles) away.

Strong tail.

121

FISH GRABBER

Some of the hunters of the shallow seas and river deltas are dinosaurs. Suchomimus is a sea-going dinosaur with a hump along its back. Its long, narrow snout gives away its identity as one of the fish-eating spinosaurs.

Suchomimus is an opportunist, which means it will take any chance at food that it gets. It will happily eat dinosaurs and pterosaurs as well as fish. Its camel-like hump stores food for the lean times when prey is scarce.

Back hump.

FIELD NOTES

Suchomimus is about two-thirds the size of Spinosaurus, the largest spinosaur.

If you're boating in Suchomimus-infested waters, never trail your hands or feet over the side. A Suchomimus could easily grab the dangling limb in its jaws and drag you into the water.

Narrow snout with conical teeth.

Head is more than 1 m (3.3 ft) long.

Suchomimus is a cousin of the land spinosaurs, such as Baryonyx.

Stout, powerful arms.

DINO DATA

SUCHOMIMUS (SOO-KOH-MIM-USS)
MEANING: "CROCODILE MIMIC"

FAMILY: SPINOSAURIDAE
TIME: EARLY CRETACEOUS
DIET: FISH

LENGTH: 10 M (33 FT)
WEIGHT: 2.5 TONNES
(2.8 TONS)

123

SUPER CROC

Deadly Deinosuchus is a killing machine that lives along coastal regions. It's a very large member of the crocodile family, and uses the same hunting technique as modern crocs and alligators. It ambushes and wounds prey, then drags it into the water.

Deinosuchus is as long as T. rex is tall!

Deinosuchus kills and eats fish, turtles, and even large dinosaurs that have come to the water's edge to drink. It has a formidable bite, thanks to big, crushing teeth in its massive jaws. It can probably even take chunks out of well-defended, shielded dinosaurs!

Alligator-like body.

Large tail.

BEASTLY DATA

DEINOSUCHUS (DIE-NOH-SOOK-USS)
MEANING: "TERRIBLE CROCODILE"

FAMILY: ALLIGATOROIDEA
TIME: LATE CRETACEOUS
DIET: FISH, MEAT

LENGTH: 11 M (36 FT)
WEIGHT: 4.5 TONNES
(5 TONS)

Unsuspecting Parasaurolophus has come to drink.

Powerful jaws.

FREAKY CROC

Simosuchus lives at the same time as Deinosuchus. It's a crocodile, too, but a very odd one. At just 75 cm (2.5 ft) long, it's rather small, and it has a strikingly blunt snout. Unlike every other member of its family, Simosuchus is a plant-eater.

Broad snout.

Avoid the water's edge, if you possibly can—and avoid the kind of thick plant growth that could provide a lurking Deinosuchus with good cover.

SURVIVAL GUIDE: DEINOSUCHUS

GLOSSARY

AMMONITE
An extinct shellfish in a coiled shell that was common in the Mesozoic.

AMPLIFY
To make (a sound) louder.

ANKYLOSAUR
An ornithischian dinosaur with defensive bony plates on its back.

ARCHOSAUR
A group of animals whose skulls have one hole between the eye socket and nostril and another at the back of the lower jaw. Archosaurs include present-day crocodiles and birds, and extinct crocodilians, rauisuchians, dinosaurs, and pterosaurs.

BREEDING SEASON
The time of year when animals gather to mate in order to have offspring.

BROWSE
To feed on shoots, leaves, and other plant matter.

CARNIVORE
A meat-eater.

CARRION
Rotting flesh from a dead animal.

CERATOPSIAN
An ornithischian dinosaur with a beaked mouth and, usually, horns and frills. Early ones were two-legged; later species were large and walked on all fours.

COLD-BLOODED
Describes an animal that cannot control its body temperature.

CREST
A body part that sticks up from an animal's head, and is usually ornamental.

CRETACEOUS PERIOD
The time from 145 to 65 million years ago, and the third of the periods that make up the Mesozoic era.

DICYNODONT
A primitive, tusked mammal.

DORSAL FIN
An upright fin found on the backs of many marine or freshwater animals including fish and ichthyosaurs. It keeps the animal stable in the water, and is also used for steering.

DROMAEOSAUR
A small theropod dinosaur with an outsize claw on each back foot.

EVOLUTION
The process by which one species can change into another species, over millions of years, by passing on particular characteristics from one generation to the next.

EXTINCT
Describes an animal or plant that has disappeared from the world forever.

FILTER-FEED
To extract food, in the form of tiny organisms or fish, from water by passing it through sieve-like parts of the mouth.

FLIPPER
Flat forelimb ('front leg') that has evolved to help an animal move through water.

FOSSIL
The remains of an animal or plant that died long ago, preserved in rock.

FRILL
A bony area around a dinosaur's neck.

GASTROLITH
A stone in the stomach that helps digestion (breaking down food into nutrients that the body can use).

GILL
Body part that allows fish and some other aquatic animals to breathe underwater.

HADROSAUR
Also known as a duck-billed dinosaur, a plant-eating dinosaur with a beak-like mouth.

HERBIVORE
A plant-eater.

ICHTHYOSAUR
A dolphin-like, predatory marine reptile that lived in the Mesozoic.

INSECTIVORE
An animal that eats insects.

JACOBSEN'S ORGAN
A sense organ that detects chemicals and scents.

JURASSIC PERIOD
The time from 206 to 145 million years ago, and the second of the periods that make up the Mesozoic era.

MESOZOIC ERA
The period of geological time from 251 to 65 million years ago.

MOSASAUR
A large, predatory marine reptile of the Cretaceous, which had four paddle-like limbs.

OLFACTORY BULB
The part of the brain involved in smelling.

OMNIVORE
An animal that eats plants and meat.

ORNITHISCHIAN
Describes dinosaurs that had hip bones arranged like those of a bird. The ornithischians were made up of the ornithopods, pachycephalosaurs, ceratopsians, stegosaurs, and ankylosaurs. They were all plant-eaters.

OSTEODERM
A lumpy, bumpy scale on a reptile's skin.

PALEONTOLOGIST
A scientist who studies fossils.

PLATE
A protective, bony section on a reptile's skin.

PLESIOSAUR
A long-necked, predatory marine reptile that lived in the Jurassic and Cretaceous.

PLIOSAUR
A kind of short-necked, big-headed plesiosaur.

PREDATOR
An animal that hunts and eats other animals for food.

PREY
An animal that is hunted and eaten by other animals for food.

PTEROSAUR
A flying reptile with wings made from skin stretched over a long fourth finger.

PYCNOFIBER
A hair-like body covering found on a pterosaur's body.

RAUISUCHIAN
A large archosaur that lived during the Triassic.

RHYNCHOSAUR
A small, primitive reptile.

SAURISCHIAN
Describes dinosaurs that had hip bones arranged like those of a lizard. The saurischians were made up of the meat-eating theropods and plant-eating sauropods.

SAUROPOD
A huge, long-necked, plant-eating saurischian dinosaur that walked on all fours.

SCAVENGER
An animal that eats carrion or leftover kills from other hunters.

SERRATED
Having a notched, knife-like edge.

SPECIES
One particular type of living thing. Members of the same species look similar and can produce offspring together.

SPINOSAUR
A specialist theropod dinosaur, around from the Late Jurassic, which had a long, narrow snout like a crocodile's for eating fish.

SUPERCONTINENT
A landmass made of more than one continental plate.

THAGOMIZER
The group of defensive spikes on a stegosaur's tail.

THEROPOD
A two-legged, carnivorous saurischian dinosaur with sharp teeth and claws.

TITANOSAUR
A huge sauropod with a relatively small head.

TRIASSIC PERIOD
The time from 251 to 206 million years ago, and the first of the periods that make up the Mesozoic era.

WARM-BLOODED
Describes an animal that can keep its body temperature the same, whatever the surroundings.

WINGSPAN
The width of a flying animal's outstretched wings, from wing tip to wing tip.

INDEX